"I, not events, have the power to make me happy or unhappy today. I can choose which it shall be. Yesterday is dead; tomorrow hasn't arrived yet. I have just one day, today, and I'm going to be happy in it."

– *Groucho Marx*

"Wow! This is the ultimate 'TO-DO' list. Follow this and you can't help but live a happier life."

> – *David Leonhardt, "The Happy Guy,"*
> *www.thehappyguy.com*

"Just shaking J.P.'s hand and that wonderful smile, lifts my spirit for the rest of the day."

> – *S. Ralph Gordon,*
> *Nashville Entertainment Attorney*

"J. P. always has a smile on his face and you can always tell there is genuine joy in his heart."

> – *Mark R. Warner, Former Governor,*
> *The Commonwealth of Virginia*

"Just the thought of J. P. and his invigorating spirit cheers my heart and makes me smile."

> – *George Allen,*
> *Former United States Senator from Virginia*

"Gus holds the secrets for true happiness. Happiness begins with a smile on your face. That smile will last forever if you share it with others. Allow this journey to begin by reading this book."

> – *Dr. Bill Magee,*
> *CEO and Co-Founder of Operation Smile*

"You will really be happy after reading Godsey's book. Lighten up your day and pick up a copy of *How To Be Happy EVERY DAY*. It will put a smile on your face and make you feel cheerful all day. It's a good thing it wasn't around while I was still playing."

— *Ted Hendricks,*
NFL Hall of Fame, Defensive End and
Four-Time Super Bowl Champion

"I've known 'Sir Happy' for the last few years. He is undoubtedly the happiest 'knucklehead' I've ever met, and on top of that a good friend." HA! HA!

— *Roman Gabriel,*
Legendary NFL Quarterback and
1969 NFL's Most Valuable Player

"Gus is high on life — a life that radiates joy and happiness to all those that he meets."

— *Thelma Drake,*
2nd District Virginia Congresswoman

"Gus's optimism is doled out in a big way, I'm talking Texas-sized-B-I-G. He is ten gallons of happiness in a five gallon bag. When I need a personal happiness tonic, Gus is a phone call — or, in the case of this book — the turn of a page away."

– Dennis McCafferty,
Senior Writer with USA Weekend Magazine

"The constant with J.P. Godsey is an assertive display of genuine friendship and a pleasant outlook on life.

We are all capable of expressing to each other these same mannerisms which seed and nurture existential benefits.

Bobby McFerrin ("Don't Worry, Be Happy") made a societal impact with a particular thought and a catchy tune as if he challenged the listening world to have fun again.

How To Be Happy EVERY DAY has the potential to trigger similar and empowering responses…for me, it's the daily acknowledgment of the beauty of nature and the unbound potential of humanity to be nice to one another."

– John H. Mills, II,
The Mills Brothers™

"Being happy is so natural with Gus because no one I know has more friends, more charity for the less fortunate and more personal integrity.

How To Be Happy EVERY DAY is a reflection of this happiness."

"I knew Gus was a happy guy the moment I met him, and when I found out he was a wrestler too, heck, it was easy to see why. Pick up a copy of this book or I'll come down and put you in a headlock like the one I put Gus in for a half hour one day."

"There's a reason J.P. Godsey was named the Happiest Man in America. His enthusiasm is contagious; you can't help but smile."

"Buy this book and give it away! It is an immediate gift of hope and inspiration. It is water in a parched land. It is a smile and cup of coffee to life's weary traveler. I have witnessed just one of J.P.'s thoughts transform a person's day in the twinkling of an eye. Pack it in your suitcase. Put a copy on your night stand. This small volume can be turned to over and over again with new insights coming from each reading. I will continue to give it away, letting it's seeds take root in hearts that need to be free to love, laugh and live again.

— Rev. Michael M. Simone,
Senior Pastor, Spring Branch Community Church,
Virginia Beach, VA

How To Be Happy
EVERY DAY

by the Happiest Man in America,
J.P. "Gus" Godsey

New York

Text by J.P. "Gus" Godsey
© 2005, 2008 J.P. Godsey. All rights reserved.

ISBN: 0-9760901-5-5

Published by:

MORGAN · JAMES
THE ENTREPRENEURIAL PUBLISHER™
www.morganjamespublishing.com

Morgan James Publishing, LLC

1225 Franklin Ave. Ste 325

Garden City, NY 11530-1693

Toll Free 800-485-4943

www.MorganJamesPublishing.com

Habitat
for Humanity®
Peninsula
Building Partner

Interior Design & Layout by:
Bonnie Bushman
bbushman@bresnan.net

Cover Image by:
Katherine Lambert
www.katherinelambert.com

DEDICATION

"Mama, this book is the culmination of all the things you tried to get through my thick head. I owe you far more than I could ever repay. I want to thank you, and I know Sue and P. J. do too, for holding together our family, teaching us right from wrong, and giving us more love than we ever deserved. Mama, I wish I had been a better son, although I hope you are proud of me now. I'll see you when the roll is called up yonder. 'Til then, I love you."

ACKNOWLEDGMENTS

All efforts in life, good or bad, big or small, great and not-so-great, there are people that are responsible. Well, I am here to say I am far from as eloquent as Dale Carnegie, or Earl Nightingale, as you will soon see. I can sing Paul Overstreet, but I couldn't come close to writing a song as gifted as he does. I can say thanks, so please allow me to do so to a few people who deserve it!

Mama, thank you and I love you. Daddy, you too. I appreciate EVERYTHING. I wish you were both still here.

Thanks Judi, Paul and Sue Godsey for sharing a slew of ideas on happiness that I would not have imagined. Your ideas I have crafted into this book. You deserve a great deal of credit for this. T.C. would say thanks too but he's fishin.' (It's a family joke.)

USA Weekend magazine and their Pulitzer Prize-nominated senior writer, Dennis McCafferty. Dennis, "my man," you are gifted, and you have become a dear friend. Katherine Lambert is the top-shelf photographer who did all of the pictures for the magazine and the cover of this book. I am grateful that she allowed me to use them. Thanks also to Jim Spore, the City Manager of Virginia Beach, and Joel

Rubin, of Rubin Communications Group. These two guys threw my name in the hat when USA Weekend came up with the entire idea of finding the happiest guy. I didn't even know it. Well fellas, I don't know about your judgment in happy guys, but I do know you are both good pals and I owe you one.

Thanks to all of the boys from West Virginia Wesleyan and Theta Chi Fraternity. Many of you are listed in this book with your "insightful" quotes on life, love, and livin.' "…Extends a helping hand to all who seek it…" You are better friends, many for over 30 years, than a man has the right to have. I hope I can always be half the friend to you that you have been to me.

Thanks to all the rest of my family, cousins, aunts, uncles, and those that were outside of bloodlines. Doreen, Harmony, Skeeter, Joel, Jeremy and Jessica — much love attached. Especially to my second Mom, Mary Godsey and other two brothers Jason and Guy. Jason, don't think I can't still whip you, little brother.

Thanks to Robert and Christine, Guy and Phyllis, Janet, Lynda, Brenda, Morgan, Dan, Koz, Mike, Dale, Gil, Diane, Al and Terry (I miss you both), Shep, Jo Ann, Ken, Rowena, Chad, Sheila, Layton, Joann, Catherine, Tom, Big Mike, Kent, Joe S., Roman, Ervin, the Hinkle Family, Bobby, Ron, Rev. Dyson, and many other friends that helped with this effort and have made my life a happier one. As I have said a thousand times, the blessing of friends is the biggest blessing of life. Sorry for those I missed. Hopefully, I have made it clear to you how I feel.

Thanks to all of the music people that have given me more happiness than I can describe.

Some of you may think this is stretching it, but those of you that know me, know you have never been in my home when there was not "good" music on. The Mills Brothers, Paul Overstreet, Dean Martin, Frank Sinatra, Perry Como, Vern, George & George, Michael Martin, the Tops, the Spinners, Teddy P., Paycheck, Haggard, and hundreds of others. Music is the sound of life.

Thanks to the volunteer groups who gave me a place to contribute. "Giving back, ends up in getting back, many times over." The Richard Hassell Foundation, Earning by Learning, Virginia Beach Human Rights Commission, Juvenile Diabetes Research Foundation (go ahead, Larry), WVWC Alumni Association, Theta Chi International Fraternity, The Neptune Festival, Erving Parker Leadership Academy, Beach Events, The Virginia Beach Foundation and now the new foundation we just started, "The MrHappyUSA Foundation." All of these organizations are doing great things, one step at a time and I am proud to serve with them.

Lastly thanks to the Lord Jesus Christ for his continual blessings.

TABLE OF CONTENTS

FOREWORD

By Dennis McCafferty

Flashback to December 2002: As a senior writer for USA Weekend magazine, I'm with PBS documentary maker Ken Burns high above New York City at the Four Seasons hotel. The both of us are having an extended conversation with Al Pacino, for a cover-story interview. A question about Pacino's relationship with his once-estranged father leads to his intriguing rumination on personal happiness:

"Yeah, I see my dad occasionally," Pacino tells us. "He's on his fifth wife. We were never really not connected, it's just that we didn't see each other a lot. But he saw the babies a couple weeks ago. He came to see me in a play. He's doing well, and I'm happy he is. He enjoys life. I wish I could say the same."

We know that feeling. What's keeping us from enjoying it?

"I wish I knew," Pacino says. "Part of it is habit. Part of it is genes.

"But we overcome these things. We start to realize that there are anodynes in life that help us through the day. I don't care if it's a walk in the park, a look out the window, a good bubble bath, whatever. Even a meal you like, or a friend you want to call. This helps us solve all this stuff in our head. I'm the luckiest guy in the world. I'm ashamed of myself because I don't enjoy it enough."

The great actor's words resonate with a lot of people, I bet: Why aren't we happier than we are? Why do we keep thinking of what could go wrong, instead of appreciating everything that's gone right?

Well, shortly after that interview, I met the "cure" for this dilemma, in the person of J.P. "Gus" Godsey. My life hasn't been the same since. And, now that you're about to read his debut book, neither will yours. His optimism is time-tested, sincere and, given all of the challenges he's faced — as many of us do, with far less buoyancy — courageous. And, oh, I suppose I could carry on with these platitudes as many writers tend to do when they get all "book-forward-automatic-mode" platitudy. But, instead, allow me to explain exactly how I came to meet up with Gus ...

Flash-forward to January 2003: Just a month after the conversation with Pacino, I get an, ahem, unique magazine assignment.

"We need you to find," my editor tells me, "the happiest man in America."

"O-kaay," I respond. "And where exactly do I get started on this one?"

Since we were inventing the wheel on this one, we thought we'd first pinpoint the region in which this person lives. The happiest man would have to live in the happiest, or best, place in America, right? So, with the help of a Portland, Oregon-based business called Sperling's Best Places (www. bestplaces.net), we found that the city of Virginia Beach, Va., is the hands-down winner.

Then, I sleuthed around the Virginia Beach environs for the most bona fide, no-phonies-allowed, happiest men there. And I put them through a series of tests: I gathered all kinds of factoids that research institutions — both academic and consumer — say lead to a high level of personal satisfaction. I compiled those factors into a survey and had our top 20 candidates mark those that related to their lives.

Oddly enough, however, Gus was NOT among those 20 candidates.

As I prepared for in-person follow-up interviews with them, a Virginia Beach contact called my hotel room. "Was just wondering," she asked politely, "why you never contacted Gus."

I had no idea of his existence, I replied. Was he on the list of people for me to consider?

"Yes, he was on the attachment I sent to you," she said. "I put him on the list last because he's the best candidate."

I flipped through my notes. No Gus. Clearly, I simply didn't download the entire attachment into my note file! (I generally just copy and paste these things, so human error is a possibility.)

"Well, you HAVE to call him," she said. "If there's anybody on Planet Earth who fits what you're looking for, it's Gus."

Within 15 seconds of my apologetic phone call to Gus, I knew she was right.

Now, just on paper, Gus connected perfectly: We needed someone who was married, active in the community, with a stable job and no extraordinary financial concerns. Yes, there was more survey-related consumer data that he scored highly on. But there was something else entirely that launched Gus off the map – the less scientific but clearly valid "Does he have it?" factor. In this case, the gregarious

Gus was a no-brainer. With every other candidate, I rush along in the conversations. (Hey, I have 20 guys to talk to, and I don't have all day to do it, right?) Upon calling Gus, however, that five-minute script I have in my head turns into a half-hour, free-flowing conversational riff – on everything from sports, to personal finance, to the Mills Brothers. (That's his favorite group.)

Normally, I'd be on the other end of the line, grinding my pencil into a pile of wood shavings, longing for the very second that I could dab my "disconnect" button on the phone. But Gus was different. This is a guy who was really thrilled with everything life has to offer. And his manner was charming and funny. He was about as far from that tired clichéd image of "happy people" as you can get. You know: Those glassy-eyed, Stepfordian dweebs who perpetually fix their face with a bright, insipid grin and say "Have a GREAT day!!" to everyone within a 100-yard radius. (Just once, I will reply: "I'll have any kind of damn day I want, thank you!") Fortunately, Gus wasn't like this. For certain, his optimism was doled out in a big way. We're talking Texas-sized B-I-G here: "Dennis, mah man!" he'd constantly belt out when greeting me, loud and proud. "How do you think people are going to REACT to this magazine story!? Am I gonna get to sit down with DAVID LEEEEEET-ERMAN and talk all about it?!"

He had the eagerness and anticipation of a child on Christmas Eve. Well, we haven't gotten him Dave's show – yet. But we sure have placed him in front of the cameras with Connie Chung and Diane Sawyer. Both of whom are instantly won over by this goofy but sweet blend of humor, optimism and happiness.

But there was more. I had him take four tests on psychologist Martin E.P. Seligman's Web site, authentichappiness.org. (You can take them, too; register at the site and take the Fordyce, PANAS, General Happiness and Life Satisfaction tests.) Gus aced them. Finally, he took Seligman's Values in Action Signature Strengths test, which tracks the human makeup that directly correlates to happiness. His overall score ranked at the very top among the 70,000 people worldwide who have taken the test.

This made my decision, based upon my instincts, a scientifically proven slam-dunk. For the months that followed, Gus and I collaborated on that cover story; have spoken by e-mail and phone countless times; shared ribs; have written together the initial chapters of another book about achieving personal happiness; and have playfully sparred on Gus' radio program. He's kept me holding steady as we all experienced one of the worst economic and stock market meltdowns in recent memory. He's made me feel better after our family dog died.

In other words, he gives you the right words (and a warm chuckle) at the exact time that you need one. What better tonic to produce this thing called personal happiness? When I need it, Gus is a phone call away — or, in the case of this book — the turn of a page.

INTRODUCTION

By J.P. "Gus" Godsey
Selected "The Happiest Man In America"
by USA Weekend magazine

Well, by now you have heard the Mr. Happy story. I will share a bit about my background. This is the bottom line.

I am sure there are happier people out there; I just don't know many. I know that I have been blessed. Somehow, I have been able to "compartmentalize" things in my head. I put the bad things aside, or the things I cannot control, and do not spend any time worrying about them. Make a choice, first thing — on what kind of day this will be, count your blessings every day, control the "Controllables," give more than you get, stay away from negative people and gossip, and smile…It really is not much deeper than that. Trust me…don't try to make it any harder than that. There has been much said and a great deal of research done trying to make this more difficult. I guess that's cool, but it ain't me.

I'm second-generation Swedish on Mama's side. Mom's name is Doris Mathilda Sandquist. My grandfather, and then later my grandmother, came over on a boat through Boston. They had 14 kids. Mom was the fifth from the last. They lived in a two bedroom house, two stories high, on 5 Abbot Street in Concord, New Hampshire. Think about that for a minute.

My dad's (Paul James Godsey) family was all from Indiana. They were a "Heinz-57 variety" family, a lot of everything, including a chunk of American Indian. We have always been proud of being part "American Indian."

My folks married in 1945. We lived in Indiana where my dad coached. They had my sis, Sue, in 1955, P.J. in 1956, and me in 1957. Just think, married for 10 years, no kids, and then "Bam-Bam-Bam." That's a wake-up call.

My dad was not very original. He called my brother P.J. (Paul James) and me J.P. (James Paul). He envisioned us as a pitcher-catcher tandem. I got my nickname "Gus" when I was 2 years old from my Uncle Dick. He told my dad there was no way he would pump his ego by calling both of us after him, so he started calling me Gus. It stuck. Actually more people call me Gus than J.P.

My parents split in 1961. We moved to Lancaster, Pa., and lived with my Aunt Middy and Uncle George who had 11 kids of their own. We moved two years later to Rockland and Dauphin Street about 15 minutes away. I was 4 or 5. This was borderline ghetto. We were the only white kids in the neighborhood except for two buddies of mine who were Russian.

We spent four or five summers in Indiana with Dad. Those were always very emotional comings and goings. Dad would come to Pennsylvania to pick us up in June and bring us back in August. I remember not wanting to go, heck, I was probably only 4. I ran and hid in an upstairs closet, crying. Dad had to come pick me up and put me in the back of the car, a convertible. Dad was smooth. He got us ice cream about a mile or two down the road so the tears on my cheeks soon turned into a sticky chocolate glaze. I was happy again.

In Lancaster and before first grade, I was hit by a car, three different times, twice in the head. Obviously I wasn't the most observant five year old. In kindergarten, I got rolled down a hill by three second grade black kids and urinated on, all because I walked out the wrong door. No biggie, just part of growing up in a rough part of town. I came home and told my Mom "I don't think I like those brown kids." She freaked and started crying.

Let me make something clear. My Mom worked three jobs and some of the ladies who raised us kids throughout those years were black. If you had to stereotype, you would think of them as "Mammies." These ladies were second mothers to me and were a huge part of our family. See, in their eyes, and mine, I was their "baby" too. One of these ladies took a rolling pin over to the school to find those boys who "rolled" me. I do not know what she would have done if she found them, but it would not have been pretty. This had nothing to do with being black or white, at least from my 5-year-old eyes. It had to do with bullies picking on someone littler than them. We were raised that everyone is equal in God's eyes, period. The ONLY color that matters is the color of someone's heart. Everyone helped each other, looked after the neighbors, and pulled their share of the weight. With few exceptions, no one needed special favors or handouts unless they were disabled or old. I still believe that way today. Anyone that hides behind something that happened "umpteen" years ago, to justify bigotry and hatred is wrong.

And that includes things that happened when we were growing up. NOBODY lived in "Leave It To Beaver's" house! What happened "umpteen" years ago is over; move on.

We moved out of that neighborhood fairly quickly after the "rolling" incident to 540 Longfellow Drive. Another 15 minutes away but still in Lancaster. Mom continued working three jobs and put us in a private school, Lancaster Christian Day School.

Dad gave us very little, if any, child support and Mom was busting her tail night and day to keep us in a private school. We easily could have gone to the free public school down the street, but she insisted. I am still dumbfounded by this, but grateful.

Mom decided she needed to get her master's degree in nursing (she already had her bachelor's and was a registered nurse) if she was going to continue to take care of us and be able to help us with college. So…she shipped P.J. and me out to Albuquerque, N.M., to live with Aunt Bea and Uncle Charlie. Sue went back to live with Aunt Middy. Looking back I realize how tough this was on all of us. My aunts and uncles having to take us in, Mom having to ask them, and us kids not being with our parents. Such is life. Mama did the best she could. She sacrificed more than anyone. It happened, it's over, we survived, we move on.

New Mexico was great. Got my first pair of cowboy boots and haven't quit wearing them since. Learned to rodeo, although not too well. Learned to fight, although again, not too well. Racism was around, only now, Mexicans vs. whites. This was something I still did not understand. Although by necessity, I was getting tougher.

I started wrestling (a sport I continued for 12 years) with my brother at Monroe Junior High, next to Winrock Mall. I remember the junior high principal busted my friends and me one morning. We were taking the shortcut to school and cutting across the eight-lane highway. This was a big no-no and dangerous stuff. I was moving back East the next week so he let me off with a swift kick in the pants. Not really; he was a good guy just trying to keep kids on the straight and narrow.

Mama got a job in Elkins, W.Va., and we enrolled in Elkins Junior High School halfway through the year. My best friend was Rex Farris and I liked a girl named Pam Douglas. No wrestling, only basketball. Let me say this right up front, the only dribbling I can do playing basketball is down my chin. My dad never understood that as he was an all-star playing basketball in Indiana and actually has a brick in the Indiana Basketball Hall of Fame.

My sis and Mom started fighting a good bit. Mom was at the end of her rope and she told my dad "If you want them, take 'em" and he said "Fine." So after eighteen months in West Virginia we were off again, this time to Indianapolis, Ind. We enrolled in Manual High School. Dad ran a pool hall in a neighborhood not unlike the one where the "rolling" incident took place 10 years earlier. Dad was divorced from his second wife Mary. They had two boys, my half brothers, Jason and Guy. Jason has three kids of his own, and is a teacher in Indy. He was ranked in the top five in the world in "extreme fighting." You can check out his fights at a Blockbuster in your town. He is nice as can be but a very "Bad" dude. Guy has cerebral palsy with special needs and lives in Indy as well.

Mary lived next to Manual High and allowed us to use her address so we could go there. If not, we would have gone to a bad school where Dad lived. Mary is a real nice, smart and pretty lady. She has taken care of us during some rough times when we needed her. I love her very much.

We moved back to West Virginia twelve months later. This time Buckhannon. I consider this my hometown. It is truly an "All-American" town and where I graduated from both high school and college.

Mom was a nursing professor at West Virginia Wesleyan in Buckhannon. Attending and graduating here was the greatest experience of my life. I am still very close to well over 100 of the men I met at Wesleyan. These are the guys really responsible for making me happy. True friends. This is a GREAT school. I was president of my fraternity — Theta Chi, and my freshman class. I played sports, and worked for a wonderful family named the Hinkles. I graduated in 1979 with a bachelor's degree in business and economics. Sis graduated the same year although it took her six years vs. my four. I still tease her about this.

Let me say this about Sue. I love her very much but I did not always like her. I realize now what a wonderful person she is and the one who held the family together, especially when Mama was starting to go downhill.

Let me say this also about my siblings. I would lay down my life for them. As I said before, I was always the "baby." Mama spoiled me. My brother P.J. has more sensitivity in his little finger than I have in my entire body and is the nicest guy I have ever met. Jason and Guy, I love them too, and thanks to all four of you for everything. T.C. says thanks too.

Well…my first job was running a club in Myrtle Beach, S.C. in 1980. I left to run a U.S. Congressional campaign back in West Virginia for Senator J. D. Hinkle Jr. in '82. (We got beat). Did PR for the Washington Federals of the United States Football League (we got beat…), got married, moved to Norfolk, Va. in '85 and started a career as a financial advisor (back then we just called ourselves stockbrokers). I got divorced in '88 and moved to Virginia Beach, 15 minutes away. Got married again in 1999 and was picked as "The Happiest Man in America" in 2003.

As I write this freehand on a 14" yellow legal pad, I am thinking "WOW, what a ride." And…I haven't really even said anything…YET!

I am going to close and let you get into "How To Be Happy Everyday." A couple of things before you move on. All of this "stuff" is how I have been raised and lived my entire life. There is no doubt,

I have been blessed greatly. This is not a "goof," a joke, or a slicked-back sales gimmick. I believe in my heart that if we all practice these "Happyisms" every day, we will all have richer, fuller, more meaningful, healthier, and happier lives.

I wish you nothing but the best life has to offer, a good ride, and as Mama used to say (I ain't making this up), "May the Good Lord bless you...REAL GOOD!"

Gus

CHAPTER 1

THE HAPPIEST GUY

He scored off the chart on every objective measurement we tested. Yet the emerging science of contentment suggests practical ways Gus Godsey -- and anyone reading this book -- could be even happier.

By Dennis McCafferty

As Charlie Brown and the "Peanuts" gang told us, happiness could be a warm puppy, pizza with sausage, five different crayons — or anyone, or anything, that's loved by you. And, although it's true that many special moments are inspired by such happenstance, scientific research contends that people actually can condition themselves for genuine happiness, much as occasional joggers condition themselves for marathons. Truly happy people are able to, for example, recall special moments and use them as psychological tools to deal with adversity. And that's just one of many skills they tap into to ensure a high level of satisfaction in their lives.

So why is this important? Because it's clear that happiness is a key contributor to our overall personal health — it's even been linked to longevity, scientific studies show.

1

With that in mind, USA WEEKEND magazine hatched what we'll call the Ultimate Happiness Challenge: Why not pair the world's leading authority on happiness with America's happiest person and see if our expert can make him even happier? Or, on a more scientific level: How can the leading expert apply his core principles to boost the happiness quotient for someone who's already as happy as a person gets? With this exercise, we explore the happiest man's state of contentedness and, as a result, discover ways we all can better cultivate happiness in our lives.

Our happiness authority is a clear choice: Martin E.P. Seligman, 60, the author of 20 books, including the new "Authentic Happiness: Using the New Positive Psychology to Realize Your Potential for Lasting Fulfillment" (Free Press, $26). Seligman is a professor of psychology at the University of Pennsylvania who has spent his 40-year career researching the emotional and mental makeup of happy, optimistic people, as well as of those who are depressed and pessimistic.

Among the many theories he promotes: Those who are best at understanding their "signature strengths" — such as a sense of humor or the capacity to love — and learn how to use them every day, in all kinds of situations, often end up the happiest. (For more on Seligman and his new book, visit authentichappiness.org.)

As for our happiest person in America, J.P. "Gus" Godsey, 45, he's a story in himself. (See "Our Search for Perfection") On a recent sunny day in Virginia Beach, Va., we sat down with Godsey and Seligman to see how the happiest guy — and everyone else — can become even happier.

Principle #1: Everyone benefits

The concept: Authentically happy people negotiate life by stressing an "everybody wins" strategy, as opposed to focusing on threats or other negative possibilities.

Godsey: That's true. Being a jerk never got me positive results. When I get bad service at a restaurant, I don't like to make a scene. I try to get the manager and say, "Hey, I love this place and want to keep coming, but…" With that approach, you can even get a free meal when you come back.

Now, this usually works, but not always. I essentially shoulder the fund-raising load for many of my charitable pursuits; it really takes a lot of time and effort. My goal is to build up an endowment so we can help, say, homeless people forever just through the interest. But the donor giving me $5,000 is getting angry at me, saying he wants it spent right now to buy coats for people on the street. I try to tell him that this will make us feel good for now, but it has no lasting value. And, quite frankly, this kind of conversation can get testy.

Seligman: Abraham Lincoln was great at dealing with tense situations with a dose of humor. A good quip or a story can defuse a potentially unpleasant exchange. You may want to apply your great sense of humor — which is a terrific signature strength — in these conversations with donors. First, disarm them with your humor and diminish the danger of things getting testy, then proceed with the "everybody wins" approach to convince them that the funds should support the endowment. They will be more receptive if you put them in a good mood first. Authentically happy people often use one signature strength to set up the use of another.

Principle #2: Savoring success

The concept: Authentically happy people not only savor good moments and successes but also tap into those in the past to help them deal with problems in the present.

Godsey: That brings to mind something that happened when I went back to my hometown 10

4

years ago. I was with a buddy getting ready to have some pizza and beer, and a guy I grew up with approached me. This guy always wanted to fight me when we were kids. He says, "Gus, you're still a jerk, and I can still beat you up." Now, my pal is wondering what the heck is going to happen. But I just told the guy, "Hey, man, we haven't seen each other in 20 years. These things don't matter anymore. Remember how much you liked my older brother? He still asks about you and wonders how you're doing." He never liked me, but he really dug my brother. It immediately put him in a better disposition. He had been ready to fight, and we ended up shaking hands. My buddy was amazed.

Seligman: Wow! I'm impressed. There was really no better way to handle that situation. All I can do is encourage you to continue thinking of ways to recall positive moments from the past to deal with difficult situations in the present. In situations like this, authentically happy people take a moment to think about things that really went well. When people say they're dreading a situation they think will be stressful, I tell them to recall three things that have gone well lately and — this is key here — why they happened, and write them down.

If the situation is work-related, I tell them to do that before they go into the office that day. If people get their confidence up, their repertoire expands to deal with the situation.

Principle #3: Social intelligence

The concept: Authentically happy people know which strengths to use and which to avoid with a particular person or situation.

Godsey: I had a real problem with this recently. I hurt a good friend's feelings, and I didn't mean to. He had done a report for his office and wanted me to take a look at it before submitting it. I thought the report had some problems, so, in attempting to cushion my thoughts, I tried to use a little humor. I left a message on his answering machine that he should not only not submit the report, he should burn every copy of it and start over. Well, the whole thing backfired. What I didn't know was that this was a really sore spot for him. He had been going through a lot of grief with this report, and he was just seeking some reassurance. He got really angry. I apologized and asked for his forgiveness, but I don't think we're over the hump yet.

Seligman: Intriguing. Usually, you're very strong in using your social intelligence. It's a key signature strength for you. But you misplayed your hand this time because you weren't aware of what your friend had been through. Usually humor works, but this time it didn't. Signature strengths can be used like tools — but a fellow doesn't pull out a hammer when he needs to drill a hole, does he? In this kind of situation, I often encourage people to use gratitude as a signature strength tool. I tell them to think of something helpful or kind that a friend did for them, and to stress that the next time they talk to the friend to repair the damage. So, Gus, consider telling him, "How could I possibly want to hurt you after all you did for me? I value our friendship far too much to want to hurt you in any way." This is a good way to earn forgiveness and restore a relationship that brings happiness.

Principle #4: Opening doors

The concept: Authentically happy people find open doors when others close.

Godsey: This is my philosophy. In my first job out of college, I ran a nightclub in Myrtle Beach, S.C. I did really well and worked really hard. I got Mickey Mantle to come to the club to get people talking about it, to make it a hot spot. My roommate at the time was African American, and I wasn't about to exclude minorities from coming to the club. Some of the owners didn't like this, and I got fired. But one owner liked me and admired the stand I took. His dad ended up running for political office; that owner put in a good word for me, and I became his dad's campaign manager.

Seligman: That's terrific. You stood up for your values, suffered a defeat, disengaged from the situation and then found something better. Often something good comes out of something bad. People like you maintain an optimism that opens doors. In your case, you didn't stay in bed, paralyzed by this career setback; you did something about it. Now that you're a stockbroker, you know that Wall Street shuts doors and opens them — many times in a single day. The immediate reaction to a sharp drop in the Dow is one of panic. But that drop often leads to an opportunity to buy a stock that turns out to be a bargain. People who maintain this perspective often bounce back quickly from disappointments.

Principle #5: Couple strengths

The concept: Authentically happy people enhance their romantic relationships by joining both partners' personal strengths.

Godsey: I'm usually good at this with my wife, but sometimes I'm not so good. I'm a big planner, and she's really into beauty. This works great when we're dealing with our gardening. I'm always coming up with the game plan — what kind of flowers and vegetables we're going to plant, and what kind of pasta sauces and salsas I'm going to make with the tomatoes. She's really good at displaying the flowers in remarkable arrangements that make the house look elegant. But I admit it isn't always something we actually put any thought into. How else can we combine our strengths to make life more enjoyable?

Seligman: I always advise couples to combine their strengths when it comes to a big vacation they're planning. Sometimes a vacation can put a couple at odds with each other: The husband might want a spring-training tour in Florida, while the wife would prefer a week of theater in New York. But instead of being at odds, couples can work together. In your case, you and your wife can combine your strengths to go to, say, Alaska, on a cruise for a week. You can use your planning strengths to find the best tour package and pick out the excursions, and you can use your capacity to love to make instant friends on the ship. Your wife can bring her strengths to the package by guiding you toward Alaska's natural splendors.

Principle #6: Finding meaning

The concept: Authentically happy people leave a legacy.

Godsey: This is my passion, something I devote so much of my energies to. My charitable efforts are geared toward helping the needy, sheltering the homeless and improving literacy among at-risk kids. It's important not only to make a difference now, but to leave a lasting endowment that will continue to help people long after I'm gone. My favorite quote is from William James — the big-time Harvard psychologist and philosopher — who said, "The greatest use of life is to spend it for something that will outlast it." That's the underlying spirit behind my thinking. Usually I can convince the donors that my strategy will do the most good for the longest time. When that sort of difference is made, it really brings me a great sense of happiness.

Seligman: I can't say anything that can improve that kind of situation. Many people wake up every morning with a gnawing fear that they're fidgeting until they die, that they'll never establish a legacy. You are a blessed, happy person, Gus. But you've created many of your blessings on your own, and you'll keep doing so in the future. That's what authentically happy people do.

CHAPTER 2

OUR SEARCH FOR PERFECTION

So how, exactly, did we find the most happy fella, anyway?

It was a combination of science, sleuthing and surveys. Then came a battery of tests and subjective analysis — the latter of which can be clinically described as the "Does He Have It?" criteria. First, to find the happiest person, we had to find the best place to live. So we connected with Bert Sperling, the leading authority on the best places in America. He has crunched the data since 1985 and runs Portland, Ore.-based Sperling's BestPlaces (www.bestplaces.net). After inputting statistics for thousands of towns nationwide that track quality-of-life issues such as public safety, affordability of homes, healthy environment, income and education, Sperling found that the city of Virginia Beach, Va., was the hands-down winner. Next, we had to find the happiest person there. We knew it had to be a guy: Even though women have been shown to have higher emotional highs, they also have lower lows. Men maintain a more consistent

11

blend of happiness. We scouted out dozens of men in Virginia Beach who, by all accounts, were the happiest guys in town.

We then gathered all kinds of factoids that research institutions—both academic and consumer— say lead to a high level of personal satisfaction. We compiled those factors into a survey and had our top 20 candidates mark those that related to their lives.

Our happiest guy, J.P. "Gus" Godsey, connected here perfectly: He's a married dad who's healthy. He has a good, dependable job as a stockbroker with Ferris, Baker, Watts Inc. and has no extraordinary financial concerns. He's active in his community and incredibly social. He digs the Green Bay Packers, Dell computers, Coca-Cola and Craftsman tools, all of which score high in fan/consumer satisfaction surveys, according to the market research firm Harris Interactive. His nearly 2,300-square-foot house features virtually all of the items that highly satisfied homeowners have, according to the National Association of Home Builders, a Washington-based industry association: an eat-in kitchen, 9-foot ceilings, a deck and an office.

As for the "Does He Have It?" factor, the gregarious Godsey was a no-brainer choice: He comes off as 10 gallons of happiness in a 5-gallon bag, happy in that big, genuine Southern way.

But we weren't finished yet. We had him take four tests on psychologist Martin E.P. Seligman's Web site, authentichappiness.org. (You can take them, too; register at the site and take the Fordyce, PANAS, General Happiness and Life Satisfaction tests.) Naturally, Godsey aced them. Finally, he took Seligman's Values in Action Signature Strengths test, which tracks the human makeup that directly correlates to happiness. His overall score ranked at the very top among the 70,000 people worldwide who have taken the test.

With that, we knew we had found our happiest guy.

— D.M.

CHAPTER 3

HAPPYISMS

By "The Happiest Man in America"
J. P. "Gus" Godsey
As Selected by USA Weekend Magazine

ALL-STAR Selections in Bold

1. Each morning, count your blessings. Really count them. Be grateful for the milk in the fridge, beans in the cupboard, grass in the yard, a job to go to, (if you are lucky) a person waking up beside you, and kids (again, if you're lucky) safe at home. As country singer Kenny Chesney says, "Yea, man. That's the good stuff."

2. **"Good manners NEVER go out of style." My Mama, *Doris S. Godsey*, taught me that from a man getting out of his seat when a woman approaches a table, to saying, "Yes, Sir," and "Yes, Ma'am," to opening doors and a bunch of other "stuff." Do you remember all of the manners your own Mama taught you?**

Well…, our Mamas' taught us for a reason and so I think it is best we follow their lead!

3. Volunteer. If you can't stroke a check, give 'em grease. I can't say it enough — volunteer, volunteer, and volunteer. Every study has shown that people that give of themselves have much higher levels of life satisfaction. Start today. There are so many in need, and the clock is ticking down.

4. "The tragedy of life is not that it ends so soon, but that we wait so long to begin it." *Anonymous.* This is almost a sad quote in a book based on happiness. Vow to yourself, today, that you are getting on about the business of living, and that means right now.

5. When a close friend says, "May I talk with you for a moment," you know you are special when that happens. Now this book will mention several times about the importance of listening, but when this phrase comes rolling out, you better have your "Dr. Spock" ears pointed at full attention because something important is coming out. Savor that moment and be a good friend.

6. **"Life is not measured by the number of breaths we take, but by the moments that take our breath away."** *Anonymous*. **I cannot add anything to this except I hope you want to live your life like it.**

7. Take pictures of your family and friends and keep them all over, on the fridge, office walls, junk drawer in the kitchen, garage workbench, etc. Seeing them and remembering that experience will always bring a smile to your face and more importantly, to your heart.

8. Give someone a tree to plant when they give birth to a child. I have done this several times over many years and it is such a rewarding thing to go visit and see both "oaks" getting bigger. It is even more special to bring a shovel and peat moss, and plant the tree for the new parents. There are few "hands-on" things in this book that will give you more enjoyment than this.

9. Make the **choice** about the kind of day it will be. The emphasis is on **choice**. The vast majority of the life we experience is based on what we believe will happen in the morning

and then following through with it. As **Paul Revere and the Raiders** sang in the '60s, "What's it gonna' be?"

10. Give thanks to God. Or if you have a different religious belief, then give thanks accordingly. Being grateful to a higher power is good for your soul. We did not get here all by ourselves.

11. "Don't let the high seas pirate your drinks." **Joe Zemaitis.** Joe is a college fraternity brother and we were with some of the other boys out on the boat when a big wave rocked us. Everyone's drinks sloshed to the side when this insightful quote came to be. In the bigger picture, I think of this often when dealing with adversity. Life may get rocky, but "don't let the high seas pirate your drinks."

12. "Happiness is often the result of being too busy to be miserable." I don't know who said this but I wish I had. I know so many people that are so engulfed in everything that I marvel. They are living a life that is full of work, meetings, volunteering, little league

games and recitals. What would they have not to be happy about. I want to be like them.

13. "The dogs bark, but the caravan moves on." Man, this is one of my favorites. All of us, I mean ALL of us, know the people that put down any constructive idea almost before it comes out. That's fine; let them. You and I know that we still make it happen, just with one less person. So we do!

14. I always want to err on the side of generosity.

15. Don't argue for the sake of arguing. Here again, just let it go. Dale Carnegie many times would concede an argument, even when he knew the other person was mistaken with a fact, simply to avoid the conflict. Why even engage the battle? It never really feels good to win like this. Just let it go.

16. **Be quiet**. Spend time each day in solitude even if you are not alone. You can be on the bus, in the car, or in a theater waiting for a movie. Be quiet. Close your eyes, if you can (not if you are driving), and find some peace in your inner you. A few minutes does wonders!

17. Go to a bookstore with nothing in mind. Just go in and browse. It never ceases to amaze me how long I can just wander aimlessly through aisle after aisle. The adventures, the new learning experiences, the latest tips or tidbits…they are all here. And while you are at it, grab something totally off the wall and go peruse it in the coffee shop.

18. Follow the three R's: Respect for self, Respect for others and Responsibility for all your actions. I'm promising myself to work even harder on the three R's today. How about you?

19. **"You can make more friends in two months by becoming really interested in other people than you can in two years by trying to get other people interested in you."** *Dale Carnegie.* **This man is one of my true heroes in life. I believe his course, "How to win friends and influence people," should be mandatory at every college campus in the nation.**

20. Go to yard/garage sales. You talk about finding treasures. Years ago I got an 18" x 12" picture of Roy Rogers (every boy's hero for

men from my age), and was mesmerized. On a whim, I got Mr. Rogers' address and sent it to him with a note saying that he was my hero and to please autograph this "To J.P. Happy Trails, Roy Rogers." Today, it is hanging in my room overlooking the water. Is that cool or what? On this note, write to your heroes or people you respect with a postage paid return envelope and see what happens.

21. Forget about revenge. Just put it out of your vocabulary. The suffering you are feeling today will still be there tomorrow unless you let it go. Remember, nothing positive has ever come out of a revengeful act.

22. Appreciate the place that you live. My Daddy, *Paul Godsey*, always said, "Wherever you go, tell the people who live there that it is one of the nicest places you have ever been." No one wants to hear how much better it is where you come from.

23. "If you always tell the truth, you'll never have to remember what you said." *Elmer W. Peters.* There is nothing worse than a liar and nothing

worse than how you feel when you tell them...
so don't, period.

24.   Always have enthusiasm in your greetings.
Now, please. There is one rule. Do not be
that guy with a whiny voice that always says
"Have a Nice Day," to anyone within 50 feet.
As much as you would like to smack them,
please don't. Be enthusiastic and sincere about
your "good morning" or "how ya'all doing."
People will believe you because you do mean
it and that makes everyone happy.

25.   Have a special glass to drink from. I have
a Boston Red Sox mug that was my late
Mother's. It makes me think of her every time
I use it. Maybe yours is from a niece or from
a great vacation or the party favor from your
high school prom. It gives you a good feeling
with every sip.

26.   Use the good china. I never could understand
why people never use the good stuff. What
do you have it for? Get it out more often
than Thanksgiving and Easter and use it.
Even beans and corn bread taste better on
your "good stuff." And, it makes for an extra

something special when someone has had a not-so-happy day.

27. **"This ain't no dress rehearsal, Gus."** *Henry Anderson.* **I was leaving homecoming at West Virginia Wesleyan in the mid-'80s and was lower than two bits in a dollar poker game. Mr. Anderson was a longtime "second father," had a wooden leg, and the absolute best outlook on life. He never said another word after those six words he spoke, and for me, it was a life-changing phrase. God did not promise us tomorrow, so let's live our lives to the fullest today.**

28. Feed the birds. Simple enough. Get a bird feeder and fill it. You cannot imagine the joy of seeing the families of birds in our yard in the morning having their breakfast. If you don't have a yard, take a walk to the park with a small bag of seed or crumbs in your pocket and see how quickly you make some friends.

29. **Smile. A smile does not cost you a nickel, but the rewards you reap from it are endless.** *Jimmy Durante, Dino, and Nat King Cole* **all sang it and lived it so…Smile, Smile, Smile.**

30. Give people nicknames. Rule #1. You can't give yourself a nickname. This is why prima-donna athletes and singers that give themselves names like "Show-time" don't count. Calling an enthusiastic neighbor's kid "Sparky," or the new home run hitter in Little League, "Babe," makes them feel special. You never know, it may stick with them for life. I got "Gus" when I was two. Go figure!

31. **Bury a hatchet. Maybe it has been bothering you for years. There is a certain someone that something is not right with. Make it right today. Today is the day to make the call and "bury the hatchet." Even if your olive branch is not accepted, you will have done the right thing, and that is what matters. And, if the branch is not accepted, chances are it will be soon.**

32. Write thank-you notes. This has almost turned into a lost art. A handwritten, personal note of thanks is the absolute best way to let someone know they are appreciated. Okay, e-mails are better than nothing, but notes are the best. It takes two or three minutes, and you know it is the right thing to do.

33. Collect jokes. Start a file. When you write someone a note, slip one in. While you are at it, learn to tell at least two good jokes. Learn them and have them down pat. Everyone likes a well-told joke, but just make sure you know it. No off-color stuff, just the good stuff.

34. Take someone coffee. If you have an assistant, get them coffee. None of us are above helping our co-workers, neighbors or fellow man. If they do not drink coffee, fill in the blank with something else. You can do it.

35. **"The greatest use of life is to spend it for something that will outlast it."** *William James.* **MY ALL-TIME FAVORITE QUOTE.**

36. Buy surprises for the office. Now, if you are in a big office, you can't cover the entire place, but maybe you can do the few in your section. Or if that is not workable, maybe your assistant or co-worker. It does not have to be expensive. I get all of my "surprises" at The Dollar Store. You would not believe the mile -wide smiles that seven bucks gets me.

37. "Destiny is not a matter of chance; it is a matter of choice. It is not a thing to be waited for; it is a thing to be achieved." **William Jennings Bryan.** Working every day to simply do our best is a guaranteed way to be happy.

38. "I like to think I am like a kite. The more that comes at me, the higher I go. So bring it on." **Dennis W. Zoufaly.** Dennis is my "little brother" in my college fraternity. This quote comes from when people go to him with problems and are hesitant to get it out. He says this to let them know he is listening. Let your friends know they can "bring it on."

39. Say you're sorry…often. Make sure it is direct and sincere. No "half-stepping" allowed. I have always been dumbfounded (although some of my friends just say dumb), with how difficult it is for some people to say they are sorry. We all make mistakes frequently. It is how we deal with them that tells people and ourselves, who we really are.

40. Make a call today to someone you have not spoken with for sometime. Call a distant cousin, your "Aunt Middy" or "Cousin

Sauna," or a friend from high school, but "reach out and touch someone" today.

41. "Gus, always give a man an honest day's work for an honest day's pay; don't ever cheat him or cheat yourself." ***Senator J. D. Hinkle Jr.*** Senator Hinkle and his wife, Maxine, were like second parents to me in Buckhannon, W.Va. In fact, their kids Jim, John, Jeff, Jan and Jill, were like siblings and still are. The late Senator Hinkle said this to me a few minutes after I graduated from West Virginia Wesleyan, the same school he attended. He slipped a $100 bill in my hand when he shook it, as my graduation gift. These words are ones I will never forget. Senator, thank you for the countless lessons of life.

42. "Integrity is not negotiable." ***Pat "PK" Koran.*** No Pat, it sure isn't. There is really little else we have in life than our integrity. If it has been lost, there is precious little we can do to find it. So the key here is be a man or woman whose word is your bond.

43. ALWAYS VOTE! There is no excuse for not voting unless a truck hit you on the way to the polls. Legions of men and women have died to give

us this precious right. Don't take it for granted. Make your voice heard. On the other hand, if you did not care enough to know anything about the issues or even who the candidates are, stay at home. It is hypocritical to just go in the voting booth to flip a random switch.

44. Get a pet. A dog or cat preferably, but get an animal of some sorts. We once had a dog and three cats. We did have birds but I accidentally left the cage door unlatched when they were out on the deck, so they are currently on vacation. I currently have a fat black cat named "Scraps," after a college buddy named "Dicky." However, that is another story. Seriously, the love of any animal and the joy they give (Rocky had two turtles, "Cuff" and "Link") is given daily with no strings attached.

45. "You can tell a lot about a man by how he treats his horse." ***Anonymous***. I remember my Dad saying this but I think I heard it first in a John Wayne film. If you have animals, treat them kindly. If you do not, offer to take care of a neighbor's pet when they are away. You will make a new friend, today.

46. "Truth is like the sun. You can shut it out for a time, but it is not going away." ***Elvis Presley***. The King. This is true. A lie will always come back and bite you. I know it has me. Being truthful, besides being the right thing to do, makes our lives less complicated, and we never have to remember what we said.

47. Celebrate your birthday, even if no one else does. Throw yourself a party. Take a friend out to lunch. Go to happy hour. It is your birthday and it should be as special at 60 as it was at 6. Note of caution: Do not break out the "pin the tail on the donkey" game after happy hour.

48. Talk to the person behind you in line. I love doing this, making a comment about a magazine on the rack, or what an interesting vegetable they have purchased. "How do you cook that?" "Do you think that would be a good spice for fish?" You would be surprised how receptive people are to opening up to nice people and you may learn something new.

49. Get a caricature made of yourself. I had one made years ago in San Diego. Actually it is the ***MrHappyUSA.com*** logo. I have it framed

and in the kitchen. You would not believe the countless smiles and good feelings I get whenever people see it and laugh.

50. "There is honor in doing your best." **Orrin Hatch,** U.S. senator from Utah. We can't always win. Sometimes the Lord points his finger at the other side of the field both at work and in play, but we all know we can do our absolute best every day. I truly believe if we do, more often than not, that finger will point our way.

51. Be patriotic. I live, and the majority of you do, in the best country in the history of the world. Now please do not be offended if you live elsewhere. Be proud of your country, too. Those of us that live in the good ol' USA, stand tall, be grateful, and always defend her.

52. While I am on patriotism, fly the flag. Get a flagpole at your house and fly the flag. I have a 20-foot one in the back on the dock, one on the front porch that goes out at an angle and a third one on the back deck. I feel immense national pride when I see "Old Glory" waving.

If a pole won't work for you, get a magnetic flag and put it on your car.

53. "Happiness is mostly a by-product of doing what makes us feel fulfilled." Dr. Benjamin Spock. In a book based on happiness, this is one of the continuing themes. The real fulfillment comes in fulfilling others and that, in turn, allows you to fulfill yourself.

54. Ask someone how he or she is doing and LISTEN. Please don't do this if you are not going to really listen. Of course, the majority of the time people will say, "Oh, just fine." Sometimes you can tell when things are not "just fine." Let a friend know you are a trusted ear that will listen and not judge.

55. Buy a Paul Overstreet CD. Paul Overstreet is one of the greatest songwriters of all time. His awards are endless. The lyrics he spins move me. "Seein' My Father in Me," "Richest Man on Earth," "Billy Can't Read," "Heroes," and many others. Check out his Web site at www.PaulOverstreet.com. I am flat out telling you, it is the good stuff.

56.	"To think bad thoughts is really the easiest thing in the world. If you leave your mind to itself it will spiral down into every increasing unhappiness. To think good thoughts, however, requires effort. This is one of the things that discipline — training — is about." James Clavell, in his novel "Shogun." I work every day to kick bad thoughts out of my mind as soon as they step in the door. Then, the next day they know not to show up at all.

57.	Love unconditionally and give with no strings attached.

58.	Share the day's events at its end, with those you love. Even if for a few moments. It is important to talk and listen with someone you love on a daily basis. I think the best time is right before dinner. Even if you are alone, you can make a call to share your thoughts.

59.	"Make new friends, but keep the old. One is silver, the other gold." *Anonymous.* By now you know how precious friends are to me. I cannot imagine my world without them. But we can never have enough. Make a new friend today and be the best you can to your old ones.

60. Invite friends over for dinner this weekend. I really enjoy having friends over. It is better than going out because you control everything, the music (what a surprise I said that first), when you eat (you may want appetizers and then wait for an hour until dinner), plus, sharing your home with your friends is an intimate thing. It does not have to be elaborate, but you fix it all. Don't have them bring anything; this is your treat.

61. Take pictures and get autographs of celebrities. I have a bunch of pics of "big shots" that I have met in all kinds of places. The vast majority of them are very nice and they are more than willing to pose for a picture or sign an autograph. Go ahead and ask. What do you have to lose?

62. "Our body and minds can take us only so far. Our spirit can lead us all of the way home." *Susan Jeffers.* Be of good spirit, and know your heart. Our spirits are our souls…they truly light our paths.

63. "A man's got to know his limitations." **Clint Eastwood** from **"Dirty Harry."** Know your limits and stay within them. That is not to say you shouldn't reach for the stars, but stay within some semblance of reason. No matter how much I want to whip Mike Tyson, if he even looks at me like he's mad, I am going to set a track record running the other way.

64. Be proud of your home. Enjoy it. It really is your castle. From a one-room efficiency, to a mansion on the hilltop, it is your place. Take care of it. You spend more time there than anyplace else. "It's home."

65. Go shopping at a thrift store. My Mama outfitted all three of us kids there until I was old enough to get a paper route and buy my own clothes. But the fact is you can find great bargains and most of the time, the store's revenue supports a good cause.

66. Clean your garage (and attic, and basement, and shed, and closet). Okay, okay, one at a time. I love the way it makes me feel when I have a clean garage. I can actually see my workbench. My tools are all in their places, and

I found that screwdriver I had been looking for since Christmas, under a stack of papers.

67. Get a good night's sleep. I do not think there is anything I can say that creates a more positive mental outlook every day than getting a good night's sleep. You cannot be happy if you are tired all of the time. Turn the TV off, get a book and lie down in bed. If you are like me, you'll be out like a light by the second chapter.

68. Schedule your annual physical. I always have mine about the same time as my birthday so I don't forget. Don't put it off, and don't forget it. Remember! Birthday = Physical. Your health is just too important.

69. **"Character is doing the right thing when no one is looking." *J. C. Watts*. This former U. S. Congressman and Oklahoma Sooner quarterback hits the nail on the head. It really makes me feel good when I look back on a tough time, when it would have been easy to cheat, or taken the easy street, but I stood tall and did the right thing. It's easy. Just do the right thing.**

70. "People who say it cannot be done should not interrupt those that are doing it." ***Anonymous.*** This goes along with the "If you can't run with the big dogs…stay on the porch and bark" quote that so many football players use. It makes sense. Folks, if you are not going to be a participant, stay the heck out of the way and for God's sake, keep your mouth shut.

71. Yesterday is history, tomorrow is a mystery, today is a gift; that is why they call it the "present."

72. Play board games. After having dinner with friends at our house, we usually get out a game, like "Pictionary" or "Taboo" or "Cranium." Sometimes we get so competitive, it is ridiculous. Of course it is always the women against the men, and is also usually the norm that the women win. It is always big fun.

73. Sit for a long time by a fireplace and just watch. Fire, to me, is mesmerizing. I can visit a thousand other lands, come to grips with inner conflicts, remember lost chances and long ago friends, all within the gaze of a fire's

glow. The "chiminea" style deck fireplaces are the best. We sit for hours on brisk nights just watching the fire, the stars, and the sounds of the night. It is wonderful.

74. Make fresh coffee every morning. It does not matter that you are by yourself or your partner does not drink it. You do! You deserve a fresh cup of steaming java as you bring on another day of this adventure we call life. Instant is for half-steppers. It only takes two minutes more for the "good stuff."

75. Listen to the carolers during the holidays. Don't just rush by; you are much too busy, not to stop. Think of that for a minute. Carolers, especially during the bustle of the season, give a refreshing outlook on what this time of year really means. Take a minute and enjoy them, if even for a moment. It just makes you warm inside.

76. Buy a live Christmas tree and put it up early. Forget about the needles falling off the week before Christmas. It makes your home smell good, feel warm, and you know and I know it is a part of what makes the holiday special!

77. Go fishing. Whether it is a line on the end of a bamboo rod (I learned on one of these and got my bobber and hook caught in the tree daily as I practiced casting as a kid; Dad was not happy to constantly "unhook" me.) or chasing blue marlin in the islands. This is an invigorating sport. Even if the fish ain't biting, it is another moment that is good for the soul.

78. "Anybody with ability can play in the big leagues. But to be able to trick people year in and year out the way I did, I think that's a much greater feat." *Bob Uecker.* I do not know what this has to do with happiness, but it is just a great quote from an all-time "not so great" baseball player. I guess the theme here is, if you really are not that good, just try to look good doing it until you get better.

79. "Man prefers to believe what he prefers to be true." *Francis Bacon*. Mr. Bacon was a philosopher from the late 1500s, and his words are still poignant nearly 500 years later. Have the wisdom to know the difference between what you want to be true and what is true. To

be able to make this differentiation is one of life's most formidable challenges.

80. "Every time I get down and out and feel like laying back with the old dead cats of mediocrity, I think of these immortal words that came to me in a hotel in Oklahoma City...I want you to take this little thought with you, pass it on to somebody else and maybe the country will be better for it...Just remember this one thing — life is like a dogsled team. If you ain't the lead dog, the scenery never changes." ***Anonymous.*** That is great! I wish I had said it myself.

81. "If A equals success, then the formula is **A equals X plus Y plus Z**. X is work, Y is play, and Z is keep your mouth shut." *Albert Einstein.* All three of the elements of Dr. Einstein's formula are essential to being happy. The hardest, unfortunately, is Z. I practice biting my tongue. It works, and the words I was going to say just stay right where they belong.

82. "Too many people overvalue what they're not and undervalue what they are." *Malcolm S.*

Forbes. I am convinced that there is something good and of value in everyone. Just because society doesn't have a big price on it, doesn't mean it's not priceless. Remember, this is the same society that glorifies "potty-mouthed" entertainers, and overpaid athletes and actors. You know you have something good, so run with it.

83. "If your ship does not come in, swim out to it." *Jonathan Winters.* Who would have thought that this zany baby-faced comedian/actor ("It's a Mad, Mad, Mad, Mad, World" was one of my favs. he was in) would say something this profound. He nails it. Go get it, today. No need to wait. The tides may be shifting.

84. "Success is more likely when you strive to deserve it than when you strive to attain it." *Anonymous.* I believe with all of my heart and soul that good things happen to good people. That does not mean that we don't sometimes get whacked around a bit, but the difference is how we deal with the whacks. Success is the journey that we are on, and these unavoidable

nuisances are but small sidetracks to the ultimate destination.

85. Go to the zoo. And take your kid, or the neighbor's kid, or your niece or nephew, with you. Bring plenty of quarters to buy corn to feed the goats at the petting zoo. If you can't get off work, plan the trip (and get the child involved) for the weekend. Again, "Whew, man, that's the good stuff."

86. "Don't mistake pleasure for happiness. They are a different breed of dogs." *Josh Billings.* This really says a great deal about happiness. We all know that an ice cream sundae tastes fantastic, but we also know what happens if we eat them every day…The key is finding the right balance that keeps us moving forward. And on that thought, I think I'm going to go get a hot fudge.

87. "The price of greatness is responsibility." *Winston Churchill.* Happy people are successful people. The price of success is hard work, expansive thinking, taking a stand, volunteering, and love of your fellow man.

Be great today, and tomorrow, and every day thereafter and life will take care of itself.

88. "...Cause I hang with such a lonely crowd, it's just me, myself, and I..." How sad. Don't be like this old cry-in-your-beer song. Isolation only brings further depression, while being with others will uplift you and warm your heart. Go make a friend. Life is meant to be experienced with others.

89. Open all of the windows in your house today. And....if you have time...clean the inside of your window sills. They are always full of "stuff," you know, dead flies, dust, a cobweb, etc. That will make you feel good, but even better is the wind blowing through your home and the fresh clean air. Even if it is cold outside, open them just for a few minutes. It is invigorating.

90. Do something mindless like play "PlayStation." Don't let the academic types in their ivory towers say this is a waste of time and life. I love to read a great book, watch the history channel and football on TV (or better yet live), but there is a peace of mind

that comes with simply doing something that is, well…mindless, such as playing a video game on occasion. Come on, it's fun, but don't get hooked.

91. Take your vitamins, every day. I am stunned at the number of people that I run into that do not take any supplements. Many times they give me the lame line, "If you are eating properly, vitamins are unnecessary." Well la-ti-da. How many people do you know that eat properly? I mean really eat properly. Yea right, me too. A "one a day" type of multiple vitamin is just going to keep you healthier. Think of it as cheap insurance.

92. Go camping. Plan the trip today. You do not need to go spend a grand in the Sear's camping section. I got a bunch of cheap stuff at different yard sales. All you need is a sleeping bag, a flashlight, a tent is nice but not required, a cooler, a cast iron frying pan and pot with a lid. Seriously, all of the other stuff is fluff, it really makes for a fantastic weekend, and the planning is half of the fun. Take off right after work on Friday.

93. Go visit a winery. These are so much fun and educational too. We actually got off of the guided tour in California, met the owners of a beautiful small vineyard, and they took us in the back and let us sample a new port that was going to be bottled in the next week or two. We had it right out of the big barrels. What fun! People who own wineries are very interesting people and seem to be very much at peace with themselves.

94. "True happiness is not attained through self-gratification, but through fidelity to a worthy purpose." Helen Keller, (1880-1968). American writer. Helen Keller would be one of the four people that I would like to have to my home for a dinner party. (And I bet she could help with the dishes better than any of the other guests.) I believe, from the bottom of my soul, that helping and serving humanity brings an abundance of happiness.

95. Shoot fireworks on the Fourth of July. These are just a blast (no pun intended). The "Roman Candles," and those balls that shoot out of the "mortar tubes" are unbelievable. I

44

love to hear the "oohs"s and "aahs." We had some last year at our annual July 4th party that were almost as professional as the ones at the county fair. Make sure to have plenty of "sparklers" for the little ones. Of course, use common sense, keep the kids back, and be safe.

96. Chase the ice cream truck. I swear, this very moment, as I was writing, I heard the song through the open window and I just chased the truck down the street in my stocking feet, shorts and a T-shirt. It was the first time this spring. I was as excited as if I was 5. The neighbors even came out, adults and kids. Everyone had smiles and giggles to beat the band. I love that tune they play. I may even have that played at my funeral.

97. Join your civic league. People not joining are a pet peeve of mine. You know the guilt you feel when you see the freshly planted flowers at the entryway to your neighborhood, or when you get the flyer about the neighborhood picnic or meeting. Someone is doing the work to make your home and mine a better place to live.

Come on and pitch in. You will do something good and meet your neighbors too.

98. "It's supposed to be hard; if it was easy everybody would do it. Being hard is what makes it great." *Tom Hanks from "A League of Their Own."* Great quote, great actor, great movie. Making the sacrifices to be the best is what losers don't do. What extra step will you take, or what will you do without, to take you to another level today?

99. Lose weight. I know, I just chased the ice cream truck. Well at least I didn't just run to the freezer. The fact is nearly three-fourths of Americans are overweight. It is killing us and costing us billions, not taking into consideration the millions of self-esteems that have been decimated. Whether it is low fat, or low carbohydrate (this is what works for me), get on a plan, get some exercise, and get with it.

100. Make a point of talking with an older person today. Preferably someone that you do not know. Listen. Ask them their opinion about anything — war, peace, politics, the hot local story — and just listen. They know so much

and are rarely asked. Remember, they have "been there, done that."

101. Shop at discount stores; it feels great to get a bargain. Every year I have a Christmas party for my clients and our friends. I have close to 100 clients that show up. For the past three years, I bought 100 tree ornaments that were hand-painted glass globes. Each came in a silk lined box with a little ivory latch to close it. As each guest left my home that evening, I gave each a box with a holiday sticker on the bottom. I have seen these elsewhere priced at $10, but I got mine for a buck apiece at the dollar store.

102. Trust your instincts; your gut is usually right. If it does not feel right, don't do it. If I had trusted mine, this book would have been out 18 months earlier. Be careful not to confuse insecurity with a deep feeling that something is not right. The old saying, "Let your conscience be your guide," holds as true today as it did 1,000 years ago.

103. Be a tutor. Helping someone learn to read and write is almost the greatest gift of all.

The feeling you will have when you see the light come on in the child's eye when he or she "gets it," is priceless. If you want a way to get started, contact the local school principal in your neighborhood.

104. Go to a high school game, or concert, or play. Cheer them on. There is nothing like high school activities. There is talent that is still developing. Of course there are plenty of errors, missed lines, sour notes, etc., but the beauty of these young minds and the future that lies before them make these events so meaningful. Plus, they so much need our support and to know we care.

105. Read the Bible. Even if your religion is different and you do not believe it, read it anyway. It is a fascinating collection, and there is much to learn about life, history, wisdom, patience, love, and being a good person.

106. Always say "Please" and "Thank you." I do not know where this common courtesy fell by the wayside. I was signing things at a junior high recently where I had just spoken on the "Mr. Happy" story. It was not until I signed my

15th program or so that a bright-eyed young lady said "Thank you." I looked up and said to her, "You are the first to say thanks. Thank you! That means a great deal to me." The other kids got deftly quiet, but everyone said thank you after that. Simple courtesies mean so much.

107. Always give credit to the ones who do the work. It makes me nauseous, really gets my goat, when a boss steals the thunder from a subordinate who really chopped the wood for a project. Besides being the right thing to do, you will be admired from everyone involved for your commitment to integrity.

108. There are only three times that a man goes in front of a woman — through a revolving door, down a flight of stairs, and through a crowded room (restaurant). Remember 'em and practice 'em. Good manners never go out of style.

109. "Tooth-Hurty." **Dicky Warhurst.** Another college pal with infinite pearls of wisdom. This crack is preceded by, "What is the best time to go to the dentist...2:30...Tooth-Hurty." Get

it? I know it is weak, but it kills me. The point is, make up special sayings that no one else knows except a few friends. When I want to meet a friend at 2:30 I'll say, "I'll pick you up at..." (then I tap my cheek with my finger). It's funny. It's cool. It works.

110. Use pet names for your loved ones. Go ahead, call your spouse anything from "Pumpkin," to "Cup-cake," to "Boo-Boo" (as in Yogi's little buddy....OK, don't get sick) and the kids "Knucklehead" (OK, just kidding on that... not really). This kind of goes along with the nickname thing we talked about earlier, but this is a little more endearing and just plain silly fun.

111. Speaking of silly, be silly. It's a lot of fun to laugh at yourself and it's healthy. Please don't take yourself too seriously. It's just not good for you. Look at the people who do. That's proof enough and really kind of sad. Tell a corny joke or learn a silly trick. Have fun and laugh.

112. If you can't take a vacation, take a three-day weekend. Go visit some old friends and stay

with them. If money is tight, forget about the expensive restaurants. Tell them you are buying the burgers and cooking out on their deck. The importance of getting away from home, reenergizing your batteries, and seeing things from the outside looking in is too precious to be denied. Look at your calendar and plan a trip today.

113. Forget the hotel, stay with family and friends when visiting. Now granted, sometimes a hotel is your only respite from the multitudes that are all assembled at "Aunt Bea's" home. When it is appropriate, it is so nice to stay up late with these special people sharing memories and dreams yet to come, without having to get loaded up in the car and drive to a motel. Plus, I love to see everybody in their bathrobes having morning coffee.

114. Listen to Irish music and go to a parade on St. Patrick's Day. Go to an Irish pub and listen to the bagpipes. It is better yet to find a place that has singalong sheets of Irish songs. There is nothing quite like sharing a pint with

a new mate and belting out "When Irish Eyes are Smiling."

115. Learn to appreciate country music. Now hold on here. Some of you are saying "gag." "You have crossed the line here, Gus." Well, just wait. Country music has some of the most poetic, heartfelt lyrics you will ever ever hear, real American stuff. It is not all cry-in-your-beer music, although granted, some is. There are beautiful words about family, faith in God, love of freedom and country. And best of all, you can actually hear and understand the lyrics…go figure. I love it!

116. Ride a bike. I have a "bicycle-built-for-two" with a wire basket in the front and a small American flag taped to it. It is more fun than a little bit. Take the whole family biking. Put sandwiches in your basket, and make it a picnic.

117. Create an "I love me" wall in your home or office. I have all kinds of pictures of celebrities, politicians, and just friends that I have framed and hanging in both my home and office. People get the biggest kick out of looking at

these and asking, "Where did you meet him?" This is something that will give you enormous pleasure many times throughout the day…get started today.

118. Give toasts. Toasting is a lost art. There are many good books on this. My favorite is, **A Gentleman Raises His Glass**, by John Bridges and Bryan Curtis. I am convinced a well thought out, sincere, from-the-gut toast is one of the most eloquent things a guest or host can do. Practice ahead. Make sure you stick it like a Mary Lou Retton landing in the 1984 Olympics.

119. So much in our lives could be recycled, but we just throw it away instead. When something wonderful happens, do we savor the joy and then pass it on? Or, do we just let the joy die without sharing? When you are feeling great, pick up the phone or pick up a pen. Send a quick e-mail. Share your joy whenever you can and others will share theirs with you in return. Recycle your very best feelings…they just might come back to you again. *David Leonhardt, "The Happy Guy."* Contact David

and he will hook you up with a daily dose of happiness delivered directly to your e-mail. He is a good guy and this is the good stuff. **www.thehappyguy.com.**

120. Be generous with praise and show your love and admiration publicly. Don't be shy to dish out the goods to recognize high achievement or acts of kindness. Everyone needs to know who did these nice or admirable things and how you feel about them.

121. Be hospitable with your guests. As Jed Clampett said on "The Beverly Hillbillies," "….Have a heapin' helpin' of our hospitality." One thing about Jed and Granny, they really tried to make strangers feel at home. Now you may want to forsake the possum Granny fixed, but make guests feel welcome whether it be a luncheon at your office or dinner at your home. Everyone likes to feel special.

122. Learn to smoke ribs, chicken and barbecue. In fact, it is important to your well-being that you become a master of the grill. My two buddies from Mississippi (both Blue Ribbon rib cookoff winners) taught me how to do

ribs (the secret is keeping them sprayed every 20 minutes with a third each of lemon juice, vinegar, and soy sauce). Smoked foods on a deck equal happy people. Period.

123. "Imagination is the highest kite one can fly." *Lauren Bacall.* Besides being the only female member of Sinatra's "Rat Pack" (for you purists, I am not counting Shirley McClain), Ms. Bacall is a very cool lady. Cool like Sinatra, Dino, and Bogie. Letting your imagination soar is the first step in having dreams come true.

124. **"Turn your face to the sun and the shadows fall behind you."** *Maori Proverb.* **Wow. This really blows me away. I wish I could think of prophetic things like that. Is it ever so true? If we look in the eyes of the good, the bad will fall by the wayside. I am really going to be positive every day.**

125. "Ideas are great arrows, but there has to be a bow." *Bill Moyers.* This is so true. The world is full of dreamers that have more wonderful thoughts than we can imagine. However, those thoughts are useless unless they are acted upon. All the good things we discuss in

this book need one thing to make a difference in life — to be put to use. Take your arrow and be a bow.

126. "I told my daughter on her wedding day, when we get to the end of the aisle, I may let go of your hand, but I will never let go of your heart." *Mickey Mantle.* Micky was a friend of mine who used to come visit me in Myrtle Beach. He really had a huge heart and gave me a pair of cowboy boots for my birthday in 1981 that I still wear today. This says to me how important it is to let your children know they are never really gone.

127. If we struggle to obtain "things" in order to be happy, our "order" of things is sadly amiss. It is abundantly clear that material things cannot give us happiness. Sure, a hot sports car, $1,500 suit and $200 champagne are very "pleasurable," but they are just that, short-termed gratifications. I believe if our efforts are noble and focused on the "good things," the happiness and the far more important "pleasures" of life will come. Obviously, the

important things in life are not material. Don't let anyone try to tell you otherwise.

128. Tell your spouse/sibling/children/partner/ assistant, they look nice. Be sincere, as everyone enjoys a well-stated compliment. And the sexual harassment foolishness is just that, foolishness. You and I, and your assistant, know that a positive and well-mannered statement such as "You look great today," is just that, a nice compliment. Don't ever let it be anything else.

129. Go to a piano bar. I love a piano bar, especially one that lets you sing along. You talk about making new friends. Did you ever notice a mean person who loved to sing? I think not. Take along a mental list of requests and take your turn throwing them out. Be sure to tip the pianist and make sure you follow the one piano-bar rule: If you do sing along, make sure it's the same song that the pianist is playing.

130. Try a new radio station. Maybe it is NPR or an oldies station (just about everybody loves oldies from the '50s, '60s and '70s). Maybe a classical, or a "Sinatra" style, or a talk radio

station to make you think. Give yourself a boost, and try something different. You never know if you like it unless you try.

131. Write a letter to the editor of your paper. Call in to a radio or TV talk show. Let your voice be heard. One of the most invigorating things in life is believing in something and then making a statement of your belief. One thing though, make sure what you are saying is fair, is accurate, and is not spiteful. Believe me; crow is something I have never developed a taste for.

132. Devise a code word with your partner to stop fights in their tracks. One time my code word was "Bulldog." All parties must respect it. NO exceptions. When someone says "the word," all conversation stops until cooler heads prevail. This has kept many marginal differences from turning into nasty fights.

133. "I'm diggin' up bones, I'm diggin' up bones, exhuming things that's better left alone, I'm resurrecting memories of a love that's dead and gone, so tonight I'm sitting alone diggin' up bones." *Paul Overstreet.* Randy Travis had

a #1 hit with this song. Don't dig up bones, especially when you are in an argument. You will say something you regret and probably before the other person can say "Bulldog." Don't do it. It is just too hurtful.

134. Learn to paint. Seriously, go down to the arts and craft store and buy some cheap acrylic paints and a couple of canvases. They have good starter kits. I know people that have gotten into this during the past year and they have become very good. From what I can gather, it is a mental vacation. I am going to try it this year.

135. Learn to play an instrument. I can play several, all poorly. I think the easiest is the guitar. Go get an old six-string at a yard sale. You can pick one up for less than $50, maybe $25. Get new strings. This is a must. Learn G, C, and D chords and add A and F as you can, and you can play about anything that was on the charts in the '60s. It really is easier than you think and lots of fun.

136. DO NOT GOSSIP. I repeat, DO NOT GOSSIP. Be the person that people know not to even

broach the subject. If they do…they know they'll get thrown out on their ear. Gossip is by far the major reason for breakups of friendships and business relationships. If you have a problem with someone, talk with him or her. Do not yell at them or threaten them. Simply state your case and allow them to respond. More times than not, there is a misunderstanding, and if it is true, a sincere apology is usually forthcoming.

137. I love e-mail. It has transformed the way we communicate. There is a list of my college fraternity brothers that is in my address book under Delta Gamma. I can click on that one address and my message is sent to over 100 of my very good friends, instantly. Get on a list of this type and start staying in better touch. A word of warning — never e-mail anything that you would not want on the company bulletin board.

138. Buy a good pen. This is a simple joy of life. I have several and I always keep a pen in my suit coat so I can enjoy writing more. Doesn't it feel good to write with a good pen?

139. "Who you are speaks so loudly, I can't hear what you're saying." ***Ralph Waldo Emerson.*** Mr. Emerson said a mouthful here. How many times have we witnessed the hypocrisy of politicians or celebrities spouting off about this or that only to be caught with their hand in the cookie jar a short time later. Talk the talk, but make sure you walk the walk.

140. "When it is dark enough, you can see the stars." ***Charles A. Beard.*** Many times we have to be at the very bottom before we find the truth that we strive for, or before the pearls of wisdom we seek are offered. Understand this and be ready to grab your telescope. The stars are just ahead.

141. "The heart of a fool is in his mouth, but the mouth of a wise man is in his heart." ***Benjamin Franklin.*** I have always loved Ben. What a brilliant and insightful man. Here he so eloquently offers the importance of love in our lives. He also said, "Beer is proof that God loves us and wants us to be happy." Do you love this guy or what?

142. "Have a heart that never hardens, a temper that never tries, and a touch that never hurts." *Charles Dickens.* Ah, but if we could all live with these three simple thoughts in mind, what an even more delightful place this would be.

143. **Maybe the best kind of friend is the kind you can sit on a porch and swing with, never saying a word, and then you walk away feeling like it was the best conversation you've ever had.**

144. The happiest of people don't necessarily have the best of everything, they just make the most of everything that comes their way. This is another spin on the "God never promised us tomorrow" thought. I know I am going to make the most of today. How about you?

145. "In three words I can sum up everything I've learned about life: It goes on!" *Robert Frost.* This renowned poet says it in his briefly best. The sun is going to rise tomorrow. You can bet on it. Whether we will be participating, who knows? What I do today may make an impact, if not for me, but for those still pursuing the dream.

146. Get started on that chore that you have been putting off since last summer. Go ahead, paint the den (at least buy the paint), wax the floor, fix the broken chair (you see it every day and it's killing you because it should have been done six weeks ago). Get going. You will be through before you know it and feeling great. Make a list now, and get started. Not tomorrow, NOW.

147. Get a good kitchen knife. Again, a simple pleasure. There are few things that bring about more immediate pleasure than a sharp, well balanced, feels-good-in-your-hand, "Let me just slice something" kitchen knife. I recently bought a fantastic lifetime guaranteed set off an infomercial from a guy called "Chef Tony." One of the knives is called a "Rock and Chop." It is awesome.

148. Mama always told me, "Son, you may not always be able to afford the best clothes, but you can always keep your fingernails clean and your shoes polished." I scrub my nails with an old toothbrush in the shower. My boots only take two minutes to do with

that new roll-on stuff, so no excuses. Don't forget to polish your shoes before you put on your dress shirt. I have splattered many shirts by forgetting.

149. **"A real friend is one that walks in when the rest of the world walks out."** *Walter Winchell.* **Oh to be a good friend. I have always said there are far too many that have far too few friends in the world. A good friend is more precious than almost anything in the world. Writing this book makes me reinforce my determination to be an even better friend to the many that I love.**

150. "Few men during their lifetime come any-where near exhausting the resources dwelling within them. There are deep wells of strength that are never used." *Richard Byrd.* This man was a great aviator and explorer. I agree that we have so much inside us that we never tap into. Only rarely do we ever witness a flash of what we have. My goal in life is to be on E and running on fumes when my roll is called up yonder.

151. "It is expressly at the times that we feel most needy that we will benefit the most from giving." **Ruth Ross.** I am convinced of this. I know firsthand that I have felt an immense sense of pride and accomplishment right after I have been at a very low level. This came about by picking myself up off the floor and making a decision to do something charitable, to be involved. It works. Trust me.

152. "It's kind of fun to do the impossible." **Walt Disney.** I think you would be hard-pressed to name more than 10 Americans (with the exception of the founding fathers) that have done more for this country than Walt Disney. He has my vote just for giving us Baloo the Bear in the "Jungle Book." I mean for the love of Pete, ya' just don't get good acting like that nowadays. Go rent the "Jungle Book," or better yet, buy it. I am on my second copy.

153. Keep a good record of things. This means taking a videotape of your home furnishings, tax documentation, business dealings, and important e-mails. The videotape is good for insurance purposes in case of a loss and copies

of your correspondence is just good business. This is also very helpful when you have your "annual employee review." You can document your contributions to the organization. You get the raise and the promotion. Plus, your boss looks like a champ for having the foresight to hire you.

154. "The phrase 'working mother' is redundant." Jane Sellman. Man she really nails it here. I've always been convinced that working mothers are the backbone of this great country. Of the many that you know, thank one today. To all the working mothers, please accept this as my toast to you. Thank you, God bless you, and salute.

155. Go to the movies, get a large popcorn with salt and extra butter (Make sure you have the refreshment attendant stop when the bag is half full, add one layer of butter and some salt, shake it, then fill the rest of the bag and put more butter and salt on top. Failing to do this is a typical rookie error). Get a large soft drink, extra napkins, snuggle up in a seat

near the center isle, and just forget. Ah! The pleasure of a great movie and good popcorn.

156. The Golden Rule always applies. It applies at all times, to all people, in all things and in all places.

157. "I always try to treat people just a little bit better than they treat me." *Mrs. Wilson as told by Curt Sinclair.* This is just the new and improved version of the Golden Rule. Can you imagine, I mean can you really imagine, what this world would be like if everyone read this phrase this morning and resolved to live it?

158. Get some exercise. OK, unless Jack Lalane or Arnold Schwarzenegger is reading this book, nobody gets enough exercise, including me. But we can all get better and more diligent at this. Walk around the block after dinner or ride a bike in the morning. Do 25 pushups and/or situps right before you shower. Anything is better than nothing. You don't have to be "Arnold," so just get started; it makes everything in the rest of your life better.

159. "The real measure of wealth is how much you would be worth if you lost all of your money." **Bernard Meltzner.** My good friend of over 30 years, **Gerri McMenamin**, and a part of "Camp Cotter" from West Virginia Wesleyan's homecomings, gave me this. Isn't it grand? There is more wealth at "Camp Cotter" (that is where my friend **Billy Cotter** sets up his RV each homecoming for all of the gang to enjoy the festivities) than I could ever describe. That is my measure of wealth. Thanks, Billy, for keeping the dream going, and to all the "Camp Cotter" crew. I love you all very much. See you in October.

160. Grow something. We have a big garden. We call it the farm. We have corn, peppers, tomatoes, squash, pole beans and more. If you have room, dig up a spot in your yard, not too big though, and grow something. If you have an apartment, get a window planter and grow herbs. Gardening on any scale is one of the most enriching things you can do.

161. Can the stuff you grow. Now if you followed yesterday's "happyism," you should have

some things to can. This is no biggie. It involves cooking the fruits of your labor, filling up mason jars, putting them in boiling water (with lids on, DUH) and voilá, you are a bona fide home-grown canner. If you don't have a garden, buy the fresh vegetables at the store. There is nothing better than giving or receiving a canned good from family or friends.

162. "Don't be a liar, a thief or the last one to reach for the check…and that last one may be the worst of the lot." *Paul J. Godsey Sr*. This is my Dad's favorite saying and it states a lifetime of wisdom in 26 words. The first two parts speak for themselves, but the last one, well, we have all been with, I can't say it any other way…cheapskates. Always pay your way and if someone is kind enough to pick up the ribbon this lunch, make sure it ain't a month of Sundays until you do the same.

163. "It's so important to make someone happy, make just someone happy…" *Betty Comden, Adolph Green, Jule Styne.* These three were the writers, but the song will be "owned" by **Jimmy Durante**. Now how in the "wide-wide

world of sports" did Jimmy Durante turn into a million-selling singer. I tell you how — the man sang as if he were right with you and had lived every word. Get the CD today, "As Time Goes By: The Best of Jimmy Durante." "Smile" and 11 others are on this. It is packed for bear.

164. Remember the five simple rules to be happy:

　1. Free your heart from hatred.

　2. Free your mind from worries.

　3. Live simply.

　4. Give more.

　5. Expect less.

165. Swing every chance you get. It is best to have a porch swing, but a yard swing is fine too. An easy to assemble yard one is $99 at a discount store; a porch swing, half that. I have one under a giant pine in my front yard, and a yard one in the back by the water. I get the paper in the morning and sit under the one in front and "feel" the morning. It is wonderful.

166. "Will and I could hardly wait for the morning to come to get at something that interested us. That's happiness." Orville Wright, co-inventor of the airplane. We have talked about having a passion for life, well, obviously, these two brothers certainly did. Even with life's "chores," a zest and real passion for life is what makes it such a wonderful ride. Grab the opportunity that today offers.

167. Be young at heart. We all grow up so fast. We were kids and we couldn't wait, then as we got older, we want to throw on the brakes. Whether we are 6 or 96, it is good to be young at heart. The love of a child, the breath of a new day, the joy of a toy, and the sound of a giggle. These are all things that make life worth living and keep you "young at heart."

168. "Control the controllables." We spend way too much time fussin' over things that are beyond our control. Mark Twain said, "Much has been said about the weather but very little done." To heck with the weather, if it rains, I'll bring an umbrella. Let's give all our best

efforts to controlling, changing and living our lives within the things we can control.

169. "Close the door on the past. You don't try to forget the mistakes, but you don't dwell on it. You don't let it have any of your energy or any of your time, or any of your space." **Johnny Cash.** The man in black said it all here. This goes hand in hand with the "Diggin' up bones" quote from Paul Overstreet I mentioned earlier. There is nothing positive from focusing on the past. Move on.

170. "Don't try to improve anybody's joke." **Steven Lord Klebart.** Actually this is from **Steve's Dad, Roland,** but Steve insisted I get one of his lines in the book. So I did. Steve is the funniest guy I have ever met and a life long friend from Wesleyan. He actually named a big golden retriever he had after me, "Gus." "Gus" did impersonations. He used to go on top of the refrigerator (with help from Steve) and pretend he was a cat. No kidding! How many laughs did that one get the boys? A million. Anyway, when someone throws out a joke, let it ride. It doesn't make anybody

feel better by telling them how to say it better. Cool? Cool!

171. Practice your speech or presentation in front of a mirror. Better yet, put it on tape and listen to it in the car. Dale Carnegie taught me that if you are really prepared for a speech, notes are not necessary. The exception being the technical mumbo-jumbo that must be referred to. You can, and should, be prepared to knock them out in your speech, and the more you prepare, the better you will be.

172. "Courage is not the towering oak that sees storms come and go; it is the fragile blossom that opens in the snow." *Alice MacKenzie Swaim.* This is one of my favorite quotes in the entire assembly. I cannot add anything to it and if I did it, would not do it justice. Please read it again.

173. Get a good stereo system with a CD and tape player and TURN IT ON. Music is the universal language that speaks to your heart, mind, and soul. Did you ever walk into a home filled with music (good music, mind you) that the person wasn't happy? Think about that.

174. Get a good collection of CDs to go with that stereo. Whether it is country or crooners, classical or rock, just put together a decent collection and play it. Music can move you, heal you, and put you in the place you want to be. Personal note: vulgar, sexual innuendo -filled rap or mind-numbing, head banging, heavy metal does not count. If that is your taste in music, okay. I just don't get it!

175. "My God Gus, it's all around us." *Staff Sergeant Robert "Jumper" Rummells.* This is my best buddy here at the beach and an Army Ranger. His head is the size of a pumpkin. He has to go into hiding around Halloween so nobody accidentally mistakes it as a pumpkin and carves it. We were driving in my old ragtop up Rt. 17 in Ashby's Gap in Virginia on a beautiful summer day. This was smack dab in the middle of Col. John S. Mosby's Confederacy. Col. Mosby was the founder of the 43rd Regiment of Rangers in the Civil War. "Jumper" stood up in the car and said this quote. He was of course talking about how 130 years earlier, Col. Mosby's men were riding horses in this very spot. I think about

that often when I say, "Happiness is all around us." And I hope it is with you.

176. Take a course at the local library or community college. I am going to take a cooking course on "Toast; you don't have to burn it every day." I love to cook. You may want to learn Spanish so you can order your enchiladas a special way when you hit Ensenanda's (my favorite Mexican restaurant in Virginia). But there are a thousand courses available. Go ahead. Start thinking today about which one is for you and enroll.

177. Dance. Whether you go to a country joint and two-step or line dance, or kick back the living room carpet and dance cheek-to-cheek to **Steve Lawrence and Eydie Gorme's** song of the same name, DANCE. I know I don't do it enough. We did it recently at a piano bar in NYC. We were the only ones dancing, and we felt like we were the only ones in the room.

178. **On ethics: "If you can't explain it to your Mother or Grandmother, don't do it."** *Glen Salow.* **The only exception to this may be the intricacies of hitting a hanging curve ball to**

the opposite field with a runner in scoring position. Other than that, if you can't explain it to your Mama, don't do it.

179. Get a copy of Aesop's Fables and read the story again about the lion and the mouse. You know how it goes: the lion catches the mouse and lets him go. Later the mouse pulls a thorn out from the lion's paw. Well, the moral is do not judge people at first glance. I have kicked myself in the teeth almost every time I have done this. By the way, read the whole book again. This guy was a genius.

180. "With the milk of human kindness there should be no such thing as skim." *Steve Johnson.* Lather it up and bring on the buttermilk while you are at it. Here again, these people I am quoting just keep hitting them out of the park. This one is really a keeper.

181. "If you want to make sure the job gets done, give it to the busiest person you know." *Doris S. Godsey.* My Mama always had a million jobs going on at once — laundry,

mending, papers to grade (she was a nursing professor at WVWC), the Bible to study, something cooking in the oven — yet she always managed to have time to volunteer, and somehow (I still don't know how), make it to my wrestling matches. She rarely missed one.

182. "Once the toothpaste is out of the tube, it is awfully hard to get back in." **H. R. Haldeman.** This former Presidential advisor was well aware of saying or doing something that had not been well thought-out. Quick words, hasty decisions, a Band-aid on a cut when surgery is needed — all of these just get us in trouble. Resolve not to let the toothpaste out until you are ready to brush.

183. Be a good guest. Don't overstay your visit, whether it is with family or friends. This means a dinner or a three-day visit. Bring something, even when they say not to. Flowers always work. Write a thank you to let them know you are appreciative of their efforts. Note to the boys... just because the

barbecue is outside, don't use the tree around the corner for a bathroom.

184. "Love your family, even or especially, the 'Black Sheep'." **Paul J. Godsey.** Yup, this is my brother P.J. Every family has one, a black sheep. P.J. was far from the black sheep. I took on that responsibility myself. Hey, somebody has to do it. Many of us may have taken our turn in that role a time or two throughout some part of our lives. Love them unconditionally. Chances are they will be back around and will remember how you cared.

185. Get a hotdog for lunch from the guy who has the cart on the city corner. These are the neatest guys in the world. They are hard-working folks with smiles as big as the sausages they dole out. Go ahead. Get it with the works and a cold soda. My bet is you will have to have another before going back to work.

186. Invent a contest for your office. In my old office we had a chili cook-off and always had about half a dozen entries. I won the two years I entered, I might add. At my new

firm we have "Hotdog Friday" or some call it "Weenie Weekend." Not really a contest, but it's cool. Starting in April and for every other month until October my office cooks hotdogs on a grill on the back patio of the building. We invite the entire building down. Nothing fancy but you would think we were serving filet mignon. Everybody loves it.

187. Organize your office and participate in the annual "heart walk." Or pick another charity or contest that everyone, and their families, can participate in. This is a fantastic way to get everyone on the same page. Host a picnic afterward back at the office when it is over or invite the gang over for hotdogs at your house. Everybody wins with this affair.

188. "In nothing do men more nearly approach the Gods than by doing good to their fellow man." *Cicero.* Whatever your belief, I think we would all agree that we would like to be more God-like in our lives. Go out and do something good for someone else today, and you will have taken another step.

189. Have a lunch picnic by yourself today. Brown-bag it and go to the neighborhood park or down to the beach and sit on a bench or grab a towel. Take your shoes off and walk barefooted in the grass. Feed the pigeons, watch the children play or the waves race to the shore. Take it all in as this really is "the good stuff."

190. I am convinced the time to celebrate is when times are the toughest. Now hear me out. When we are troubled, just got fired, things aren't going well — that is the time we need a boost. Get out the good china, break out the steak and a bottle of wine. Gather the family around. I know that these things will uplift everyone's spirits and cause a "breakout" to good times ahead.

191. "If the grass looks greener on the other side of the fence, stay at home and fertilize." I invented this thought (although I am sure a million others have as well) when I left one position and went to another that I was convinced was the Garden of Eden. NOT! If you think things are bad where you are, chances are they will

be worse somewhere else. Figure out what is not working where you are and fix it. And then you'll be barefoot in the park.

192. Take the family out for ice cream. Or bring the office ice cream in the middle of the afternoon. There are few absolutes in this world, but ice cream is GUARANTEED to make everyone happy. Even the cranky guy down the hall or a snippety daughter can't help but be loving life with a big ol' double dip of chocolate chip in their hands.

193. Groom your dog or whatever animal you have. Obviously this is difficult with goldfish and turtles although cleaning that muddy water they are in would not hurt. Animals love to be groomed. I have had many dogs that could sit all day while I use a currycomb and literally take a dozen bags of fur off of them. It is such a wonderful way of communicating with these creatures that love you so much.

194. "You don't build a reputation on what you are going to do." This was my campaign slogan when I ran for Republican Party chairman. I served a couple of terms here in Virginia Beach.

I hear all of the time — I am sure you do too — from people spouting off about the great accomplishments they intend to do. Well, that's enough of the dishin,' so let's get on with the getting to it. A solid reputation is sure to follow.

195. Spend time on the water. Go swimming. Learn to paddle a canoe or row a boat. It can be a lake or mountain stream, an ocean, or a pond. Water is magic. Go to it often. It will reward you.

196. "It is our choices…that show what we truly are, far more than our abilities." *J. K. Rowling.* This is from "Harry Potter and the Chamber of Secrets." First of all, these are great books and fascinating movies. Make a choice to change one thing about your life. Start to exercise, start a book, finish a project, go to church, or join a club. Think of this, this a.m. and "choose" to do something by this evening. It will change your life for the better.

197. Go to the library and check out a book on tape or CD. I am addicted. I do not go on a trip unless I have several. Some are old comedies like "Jack Benny" or "Abbott and

Costello," some educational like "The One-Minute Manager," and some adventure or history. I think the adventures are the best because they lure you in so deep; the trip is over before you know it. You can learn so much from the time in your car.

198. Recycle. If you do not do it, it is unfortunate. I go to people's homes all of the time and they do not. They all say the same thing, "I know I should but I just don't." How lame is that? They are making a choice not to do something that helps us all. We are very fortunate where we live to have one big blue can that we can throw all our recyclables in and it gets picked up every other week. But even if you have to keep a can out in the garage (like we used to), please recycle. It's just doing the right thing.

199. Go to your high school reunion or college homecoming. I have never missed a college homecoming since 1972 when I was a sophomore in high school. Since Mom taught at WVWC I just walked up the street and was there. Now it takes a little more planning, but there is nothing better than seeing all of my friends on a cool fall

weekend in my "Home Among the Hills." Even if you can only drive down for the afternoon, just do it. This, again, is "the good stuff" of life. Don't let it pass you by.

200. Start a wish list. I have hundreds of wishes and dreams on mine. Silly stuff and big stuff like go to the moon, go to the Super Bowl, write a book (I can check that off now), catch a game at every major league baseball park, learn a foreign language, go to the Kentucky Derby, take a Mediterranean cruise, and run for political office. Once you have committed it to paper, that is the first step in making a wish come true. Start one today.

201. All of us want to save the world, solve world hunger, find a cure for aids, have 2% body fat and shoot a 70 in golf. Well, maybe we will eventually do all of those things, but how about if we just start out today with saving the office, or the neighborhood, or our families. Let's just take one step toward making things around us better.

202. It wasn't just the "Cowardly Lion" who needed courage; all of us do. Courage has

never been easy. It is tough standing up to the school yard bully who wants your lunch money or the guy in the office who stole your idea and claims it as his own. It is the right thing to do, and if you do not make a stand, it will repeat itself, only worse. Don't be mean. Be assertive, levelheaded, and firm.

203. Quit swearing. My father used to call it a "potty mouth." There are few things that upset me as much as continual swearing, especially the mother of all swear words that begins with F. It floors me when in mixed company someone uses that word. I usually say something like "Come on, man. Not in front of the ladies." Not to make myself look so holy, but out of respect for the ladies present. Just make a choice to clean up your language today, and don't tolerate that kind of language around you.

204. Get season tickets to a minor league ball team. We have tickets to the Norfolk Tides AAA Baseball Club, 10 rows back from the first base dugout. If you miss a game, you can exchange your old ticket for a general

admission ticket to any other game. It is the best entertainment value going. The owner's name is Ken Young. We share seats with the friends that sit all around us. This is great family fun. Thanks, Ken.

205. "One of the deepest secrets of life is that all that is really worth doing is what we do for others." **Lewis Carroll.** Ah! "Through the Looking Glass." Mr. Carroll was not imitating the Mad Hatter when he delivered this phrase. The beauty of it is that it is not a secret. If we go forth each and every day to make someone smile, our lives will be overflowing with joy.

206. "When in Rome, do as the Romans do." Half of this is courtesy, half common sense, and the other half just fittin' in. This is also a line from a great **Dean Martin** song called "An Evening in Roma." When you're in Texas eat the chili, Boston the scrod, and don't forget to tell 'em it's the best ever.

207. You reap what you sow. How many times did our parents tell us this? **Paul Overstreet** has a song called "Sowin' Love." Get a copy and listen. It says what I could not begin to.

Bitter seeds will bring a hardened heart, but seeds of hope, peace, joy, and love will reap a bountiful harvest.

208. "Offer encouragement." *Jackie Robinson.* The first Black American to play major league baseball, when being inducted into the Hall of Fame, claimed Pee Wee Reese saved his life and career with words of encouragement when the crowds were the most hateful, and he was at his lowest. What future "Hall of Famer" are you going to move today?

209. "If there is something to gain and nothing to lose by asking, by all means ask." *W. Clement Stone.* Ask, ask, and ask! Be inquisitive, want to know, and politely question. I ask everybody everything. The Q and A in the lecture, the taxi driver with the thick accent, "Where are you from?" to the toddler in the shopping cart behind me, "What is your name?" People are just fascinating and life is full of answers waiting to be given.

210. Listen to *Paul Harvey* every chance you get. He has been a hero of mine since I was a schoolboy and is on my wish list of people I

plan on meeting someday. I think I will send him a copy of this book. He is the most positive person I have ever heard. In fact, most of the time when he reports unemployment figures, he states the percentage of us that are working. Is that cool or what? There is a good chance he is on some station in your area three times a day. Check him out.

211. There is no "I" in the word "TEAM." Although my buddy *Greg Mezzacapo* used to say "yea but there's a M-E." Being a team player makes the entire organization look good and brings about more victories and successes than if we go it alone. An insightful coach or company president realizes all aspects of the team (from the guy who sweeps the floor to the star fullback), are equally important.

212. Use cloth napkins at dinner. This was a new one for me. It is a very southern tradition. I was surprised when I realized that cloth napkins were used over fish sandwiches at dinner. For you Yankees, dinner is lunch in the South, and supper is your evening meal. It took me a while to get it. I was used to paper

napkins except when company visited. But now, I like it a lot. It just makes everything taste better. They don't turn all meals into steaks, but this simple thing just makes life, at mealtime, more enjoyable.

213. Light candles. We recently had dinner with other good friends. The hostess had put small candles in the windows so we saw them when we drove up. How elegant! This little thing made the entire evening even more pleasant, and made us feel very special.

214. Learn to trust people at their word, unless they have proved untrustworthy. Of course, you aren't going to let someone take care of your kids unless you know them, but with the simple things, just accept people at their word. There is enough cynicism in life than to add another log to the fire by lacking trust. Nine times out of 10 you will be rewarded by it.

215. Become the town's master at something. Maybe it is gardening, maybe magic, maybe throwing parties, maybe healing a heart or fixing a car. I am known as Mr. Happy. People know that they can always count on a smile

and "Hey, how are you pal," when they see me. What is your trademark? Whatever it is, let that be a mark of excellence for which you are known.

216. Go to a drive-in. How much fun are drive-in movies? Is there one near you GO...tonight! Take the kids. They can sleep in the back. If there is not one, get on the Internet and find one that is close to you. If you have to drive and spend the night, do it! It will be an adventure.

217. "You plant your fields, and then you pray for rain...you hope for the harvest...then the long cold winter...and then you plant your fields again." **Dan Seals**. He was originally part of the '70s pop music group "England Dan and John Ford Coley" (they had some great hits). The song is called "You Plant Your Fields." It is on his 1985 album "I Won't be Blue Anymore." My Dad heard this in the mid-'80s as we drove from Indy to Laport, Ind. He said, "Son, there is nothing truer than that about life." It was a bonding moment.

218. Use lamps, not overhead lights. Overhead lights are for classrooms, gyms and the office. In your home, sidelights give a glow of warmth. An invitation if you will, for all to come in, "all are welcome here." That, my friend, is what all of us need after a long day at the office.

219. Here is a great one that has been around the barn a time or two. Supposedly it came from a 92 year-old lady. "Old age is like a bank account... you withdraw what you put in... so my advice to you would be to deposit a lot of happiness in the bank account of memories."

220. Polish your silver. What? If you don't want to, then get rid of it. You can't use it unless it is polished, so why have it? I always do mine before a big event I am hosting. I just jump in and get it done. Come on, the new polishes make this a breeze and it gives you a great sense of accomplishment. Plus, it's good to break out the good stuff for company.

221. Appreciate antiques. This was very tough for me. My Mama had a lot of them and I thought

they were junk. Just didn't like 'em. I wanted a new "fake leather" couch and a veneer table. Ah, the follies of youth. I learned, albeit late, the beauty of things that have stood the test of time.

222. Play horseshoes. I actually installed "regulation" pits (I use that term regulation loosely) at my home. They are the right distance and will work out just fine for a few of the boys (and girls) to chew the fat, solve the world's problems, and throw a shoe. Truly a great All-American backyard game.

223. Drive on the two-lane road on your next trip. "Get your kicks on Rt. 66." **Nat King Cole** knew, and we all really know, it just seems we are always too hurried to get to where we are going. Where are we really going? Take a different path to work today, if Rt. 66 ain't around.

224. Go to a "Mom & Pop" hardware store. The big "superstores" are very exciting and I could spend the better part of a day and a month's paycheck in one if Mama didn't have chores for me to do. But the small ones have a certain

something that the big ones lack. "Mr. Hurley," at the store he took over from his daddy, about half the size of a basketball court, knows your kid's names and how to fix any problem you have. Give him a shot first.

225. I learned that if someone says something unkind about me, I must live so that no one will believe it.

226. Eat at "Mom & Pop" restaurants. This is especially cool when you are traveling. Just look for one of those joints that have that "Mom & Pop" look. Sure, sometimes you come out with a case of heartburn that will work you over until bedtime, but it was worth it.

227. **"Don't cheat that man in the glass."** *Jimmy Dean.* **Yep, that's right, the sausage king made it. This is from his CD "Inspirational Songs." The one whose verdict that matters most is the one looking back at you in the mirror. Plenty of folks will give you pats on the back and tell you that you're swell, but you know more than any other. Be honest with yourself. Are you the type of person**

you want to be? Don't cheat that man in the glass.

228. "It is good to dream, but it is better to dream and work. Faith is mighty, but action with faith is mightier." *Thomas Robert Gaines.* The greatest plans in the world are worthless without character, vision and discipline. What separates greatness from mediocrity is getting up and making it happen.

229. Get your eyes fixed. This was the greatest gift I have ever received. I detested my glasses and this was a birthday surprise. I can now see the alarm clock in the middle of the night, see the players' numbers on their jerseys, and see the traffic signs during my time on the road. Our sight is so precious. It is worth every penny. Ditch the glasses and you'll love it. *Dr. Doug Rampona* here in Virginia Beach is the best.

230. Start a gift box. This is something that I started years ago. I have a big box of assorted gifts that I keep in the garage. Whenever I go somewhere and have a last-minute event that requires a gift, I have the bases covered. When shopping, if there is a bargain, something that

is really cool, I buy three or four. If you like it, chances are someone else will, and it will mean even more to them if you have one too.

231. "Good manners make any man a pleasure to be with. Ask any woman." *Peter Mayle*, British author. This goes back to an all star quote, number 2 in this book, "good manners never go out of style." My Mother said that. It's a gem and speaks for itself.

232. Dress up for Halloween and for any costume party you are invited to. Whew, I have done some wacky costumes in my life. My roommates, Beak, Harpo, Mezz and me used to host our own, "invitation only" Halloween party in college. One year we all picked out silver tux's at the theater department and dressed alike. We looked like "Disco Dorks." The bottom line, it's just fun and offers a chance to be silly. And while we are on Halloween, give out the good stuff to the kids. A piece of hard candy is half-stepping, but certainly better than people who leave their porch lights off. It's Halloween; get in the game.

233. I mentioned earlier in the book some things my mother taught me. Here are three more things she said worth their gravy.

1. My mother taught me to appreciate a job well done. "If you're going to kill each other, do it outside. I just finished cleaning."

2. My mother taught me about envy. "There are millions of less fortunate children in this world who don't have wonderful parents like you do."

3. My mother taught me wisdom. "When you get to be my age, you'll understand."

God bless moms.

234. Put a wreath on your door for each season. Think about it. How nice is it to come home to a "seasonal" wreath on the door? Like a fire, or candles, or nice music, or more importantly, a home full of LOVE, this is a little thing that makes a difference. Stop by the craft store today and pick one up.

235. "I'm building a ship. You probably think I am crazy." ("Well, yes, I do," is the usual response.) "I live on the river and I know you

didn't see any cranes when you came in. The ship I'm building doesn't need a crane. It is a strong ship of *Friendship*, a *Relationship* and *Fellowship.*" *David "Harpo-Big Daddy" Callahan.* Another WVWC grad and fraternity brother of mine. Dave runs one of the truly last great "All-American Mom & Pop" stores in the country, *Clair-Mac Sales* in Pt. Marion, Pa. This is the kind of store where $25 down-$25 a week, a handshake and your word can get you a house full of furniture delivered...TODAY. He looks his customers in the eye and gently squeezes their hand and says the quote from above. David is the kind of man and shipbuilder I want to be. David, your picture is listed in Webster's dictionary under the words, "real friend."

236. Go to a pet store and just browse. This is a "something-something," that makes me happy. I love looking at the fish, the iguanas, the guinea pigs, rabbits, kittens, and on and on, even the snakes. It is like the zoo. Who knows, you might end up being best friends with a boa as opposed to wearing one.

237. Lie in the sun. This is a prerequisite to being happy. If you have to put the "gook" on so be it, and that is probably smart with all of the skin problems developing. I would dare anyone to name a better feeling than the warmth of the sun on your face. From your head to your toes, it feels good.

238. Support as many of the "Oyster Roasts," "Pancake Suppers," "Bar-B-Q's," and "Ramp Feeds" (you can tell I have some West Virginia in me) as your pocket will allow. Here in Virginia Beach, we have about six hundred thousand of them. They are all great, for a great cause, and always attended by nice people. Better yet, volunteer for one.

239. "Worrying is like a rocking chair. It gives you something to do, but doesn't get you anywhere." *Nathaniel "Skeeter" Godsey*. This is from my brother, P.J.'s oldest son. This was actually the last quote to make the book. This is as solid advice as you can get and…from a 23-year-old. Please stop worrying. It will only send you to an early grave.

240. Eat outdoors as much as possible. Either a café on the street or on your deck, food tastes better outdoors. It is wonderful. It is marvelous. It's the real mamba-jamba.

241. "Life is not a video; you can't fast forward over the bad parts." **Paul J. Godsey Sr.** Where did this philosophy come from? My Dad, a graduate of Indiana State University. It fits. We can't. We must accept the bad times and learn from them and move on. I wish he were still around; I would ask him about this and life.

242. Love, worship, enjoy, and spend time with your parents. Yea, maybe they weren't the best, or maybe they were. Who knows? We're big kids now. The past is the past. My Dad smacked the heck out of me, and I probably only got half of what I deserved. Mama and Daddy aren't going to be around that long. Spend time with them. **NOW!**

243. Don't half-step. Now two-steppin' is okay (**Clint Black's** "A Better Man," and **Mark Chestnut's** "Your Love is a Miracle" are two of the best Texas two-steppin' songs I have ever heard), but don't half-step life. If there is one

thing I have learned; it is half-steppin' always leaves you half full, half done and mad at yourself for, well, "half-steppin'."

244. Skip a meal (or better yet, fast for a day). The benefits are twofold. It gives you the feeling of what it is like to go hungry. Secondly, it reinforces our understanding that many people in the world are that way every day. It also makes us appreciate the abundance we have here at home. Also, it is well documented that an occasional fast is very healthy.

245. Read the paper and watch the news. I am not saying you have to be *Walter Cronkite*, but it will make you feel better and will improve how you are perceived by others if you are informed.

246. Pursue achievable goals. Not doing this is a sure-fire way to a bummed out day, discouragement, and giving up too soon. The mistake is setting goals so far above your head that you get a nosebleed looking at them. Sure, there is nothing wrong with wanting to be president, but you might need to focus on graduating from school, or paying the

mortgage, or taking care of your family first. The presidency will wait for you.

247. "On your worst days, be good. And on your best days, be great. And on every other day, get better." ***Carmen Mariano.*** Wow! That is a fantastic statement and just made me feel better as I wrote this. We can all do these if we want to. You and I will all be better off following this phrase.

248. "Get along with the rich and the poor, the beautiful and the ugly." ***Susan Godsey.*** This is my sis's quote and our father pulled this off like a master. He could charm the country club set at an afternoon tea and be spitting sunflower seeds that evening with the farm boys when he coached baseball back in Indiana. Chances are if you treat all folks equal and good, they in turn will treat you the same. You will be the person known as being able to get along with everyone, and to be able to fit into any situation.

249. Maintain a youthful spirit. Think of all of the sayings that talk about being young at heart. Those are some pretty smart people that are

singing those tunes. They also are happy, fulfilled, and energized. They are people energized about life. Think young, and you will be young at heart. That's half the battle.

250. Be the first one to cut the tension between two people where you are also in on the conversation. I think the best way to do this is with humor. Now, you don't have to crack a joke, but a quick-witted line, directed at yourself or some other incident, will usually allow for cooler heads to prevail. You will get things moving and be seen as a peacemaker.

251. Learn to speak in public. This is a huge confidence builder and will enable you to move into circles with greater confidence than you could imagine. You can start by practicing in your car on the way to work this a.m. Just make a mental outline of a subject you know well and give a 10-minute speech on it. The most important things to remember are to know it down pat, use humor, and BREVITY. Leave 'em wanting ya' back.

252. "Everybody has talent at 25. The difficult thing is to have it at 50." *Edgar Degas.* You have

the world on a string at 25, but many people, when they reach 50, see that life did not deal the cards the way they had expected. To still have a sparkle in your eye, a spring to your step, and a snap to your appearance when we get older is a talent. This single thing tells all who see us, we still relish life.

253. "Life is short. Forgive quickly. Kiss slowly. Love truly. Laugh uncontrollably. Give freely. And, never regret anything that made you smile." **Deloris Kosciuszko**. Thanks Koz.

254. "There always be a honky-tonk with a jukebox in the corner..." *Randy Travis.* This is a great song from one of Randy's early CD's (we called them albums back then). I am a big lover of finding a honky-tonk when I am visiting somewhere. These are just good ol' boys' and girls' joints that serve great food, and have a jukebox that you can kick on the side if you run out of quarters. These places hold some of the best people you'll ever meet. Find one in your town today.

255. When someone was once asked, "Who would want to live to be 100?" I heard a fellow remark

"Everyone that is 99." I wish I had said that. There are a lot of people coming up with witty things every day, where do they get that stuff? I really am enjoying life so fully that I hope I live, in good health, to 100. I hope to see you there.

256. "Life breaks us all, some of us get stronger at the breaks." *William Shakespeare.* **This is one (of a bunch I already quoted), of the absolutes in life. We grow emotionally and mentally through the rocky roads. Nobody gets stronger when your back is getting patted. Just dig in and dig out. We will all be better**.

257. Deal with the hard times and move on. I was with my good friends, *Bob and Deloris McClish* when my assistant came into my office paler than a December tan and said, "Excuse me. You have an emergency call." Well, it was my sister-in-law Doreen who said, "Mama died." I still miss her, but there is only so much hurting she would permit. Deal with loss, and get back in the saddle. Easier said than done? Maybe. The alternative is missing out on today. Get back in the saddle.

258. "There ain't no easy horses, but you got to learn to ride." ***Written by Schulyr, Knobloch and Schlitz, and sung by Schulyr, Knobloch and Bickhardt.*** My brother Paul's all-time-favorite song. He actually has his kids stand up to sing it. Think, I mean really think, about this song title! Who is going to make you stay in the saddle of life? Nobody but you can keep you up there. Life is a ride to love. It's tough to learn, and there ain't no easy horses.

259. Do your favorite thing…and then repeat it. So many people think it's immature (side note… who in the heck gave these people the right to define immature?) to have fun. Spending the currency of life that we have been blessed with and enjoying ourselves is a chunk of how life is meant to be spent.

260. Be consistent! Waves are for surfing. Our lives and our character should be rocks of stability. As long as it is good and genuine, stability and consistency are the epitome of what is real.

261. If nobody else loves you, at least love yourself. Ya' gotta' love yourself or at the least the person

you are working to become. If you are truly a good person, don't doubt your self-worth.

262. L.O.V.E. You know love is a cool thing. It took me a long time to understand the significance and power of that word. I truly love my fellow man. "It starts,"…with that statement.

263. If the house is a rockin'…Don't bother knockin'… (for the rookies in the group, this means just come on in, you're welcome here). Jump in. The water's fine. Do something off the wall today. If you never go out to lunch with the girls, go today and try the sushi. Ask the new neighbors over for dinner. Go on. Try whatever! Life's clock is ticking!

264. Here's one on the house: Celibacy can be a choice in life, or a condition imposed by environmental encounters: While attending a Marriage Encounter Weekend, David and his wife, Christy, listened to the instructor declare, "It is essential that husbands and wives know the things that are important to each other." He addressed the men, "Can you name and describe your wife's favorite flower?" David leaned over, touched Christy's arm gently and

whispered, "Pilllsbury All-Purpose, isn't it?" And thus began David's life of celibacy.

265. "Dedication, self-control, cooperation, and always doing your ABSOLUTE!" *Johnny Wooden.* He is known as the "The Wizard of Westwood," and greatest college basketball coach in the history of the game. He recruited my father, from Rolling Prairie High School in Indiana, to play for him at Indiana State before he went to coach at UCLA. A great American! These were his priorities, and they were crystal!

266. Be the first one to call someone on his or her birthday. My college roommate, and friend of 30 years, *Greg Mezzacapo's,* mom's birthday is the same day as mine, November 1st, "All Saints Day." You got to believe God has a sense of humor with me being born on "All Saints Day." I always call *"Mrs. Mezz"* this day. She just turned 78. It is always a real cool call.

267. "Some days you're great, and some days you are just okay." *Coach Guy Hyatt.* Guy is another great friend from right here at the beach and the head baseball coach at Bishop

107

Sullivan HS. He told this to his players after they "under played" and subsequently got whipped by a team they should have easily beaten. I related to this immediately. No one can be on the absolute top of his or her game every day. This is not to say any of us should accept mediocrity, but we need to accept the fact that some days are simply going to be better than others. Tomorrow's gonna' be another day. By the way, this is the title to a big hit from the "Monkees" first album in 1966, just to keep you on your toes.

268. Talking with a kid under 10, I mean really carrying on a serious conversation with them, is a happy experience in itself. *Art Linkletter* (as did *Tammy Wynette* in a great song) said "kids say the darnedest things." It really is a great feeling, to have a one-on-one with a child explaining their philosophy on everything from cooties and cookies, to broccoli and good night stories. Here again, "Yea man, that's the good stuff."

269. Making people feel safe is a gift. Someone is on the verge of breaking down, and all that-that

entails. How rewarding is it to have someone call you, or come into your home because you are that person they can count on, that they trust, and that they feel safe to confide in. That is a gift. Nurture them, hold them, and give them the strength to carry on. You have all it takes!

270. SHUT UP! Come on, you know the drill. If you really want to be happy, you have to learn how to bite your tongue, keep your mouth closed, clam up, and shut down the pie hole. I know I wish I could take back many of the hurtful, fly off the cuff, things I have said in my life…many times to the people that loved me the most. I can't! Hurting someone with a sharp word cuts right to the bone. Starting today, I am vowing never to do it again.

271. You don't have to be rich to feel rich. What is rich? Seriously, my family was the richest in our lives when we had "hard candy Christmases." There is no gold, frankincense or myrrh that could have made me feel any richer than those times. Appreciating the richness of the love of family and friends,

and what we have, is the biggest secret of real happiness.

272. Know when to back off. Clowning around, joking, or as the boys like to call it, "goofin'," is a way of life for me. "Goofin'," however, has landed me smack dab in the middle of hurt feelings, and uncomfortable situations. Really enjoying your friends and life means taking a chance playing a joke now and then. The real deal, however, is knowing when a "goof" has gone too far and **immediately** taking care of it. Then you will truly be the "goofmaster."

273. "Drinking from a Saucer." *Jimmy Dean.* This is another song from the album called "Inspirational Songs" by the actor and sausage king himself. I would strongly encourage you to buy it. Mr. Dean talks about drinking from his saucer because his cup has overflowed. Wow! That is when the blessings of life, whether they are greens and fatback, or surf and turf, are so appreciated. I hope that all of us are drinking from our saucer every day.

274. Optimism will keep you healthy and happy. Study after study has been done on this and

they all have the same punch line: People that report higher levels of optimism are 55% less likely to die from any cause and 23% less likely to die from cardiovascular-related causes than people with sour dispositions. That in itself is reason enough to look for the sunny side of the street in every path we take.

275. **"I, not events, have the power to make me happy or unhappy today. I can choose which it shall be. Yesterday is dead; tomorrow hasn't arrived yet. I have just one day, today, and I'm going to be happy in it."** *Groucho Marx.* **<u>THIS IS THE MVQ (Most Valuable Quote) OF THE ENTIRE BOOK.</u>**

276. "Try to make at least one person happy every day. If you cannot do a kind deed, speak a kind word. If you cannot speak a kind word, think a kind thought. Count up, if you can, the treasure of happiness that you would dispense in a week, in a year, in a lifetime." *Lawrence G. Lovasik.* As *Jimmy Durante* said previously and now here Mr. Lovasik, making someone happy will manifest itself as a light on our faces for all of the world to see. That is happiness in and of itself.

277. "The truest greatness lies in being kind, the truest wisdom in a happy mind." *Ella Wheeler Wilcox*. As I have stated many times throughout this book, giving to others is one of the biggest elements of a happy life. What I have not said is, it is well-documented also, that a mind at peace and full of rich pure thoughts is much more capable of making sound decisions.

278. "Always keep that happy attitude. Pretend that you are holding a beautiful fragrant bouquet." *Earl Nightingale.* I could finish the book with all of the inspirational sayings of Mr. Nightingale. What a wonderfully magnificent man. My other favorite of his is "We can let circumstances rule us or we can rule our lives from within." Please take some time to read about this man. Anything I could ever say about happiness and having enthusiasm in life, Mr. Nightingale already has said, only better.

279. "Happy is the person who not only sings, but feels God's eye is on the sparrow and knows he watches over me. To be simply ensconced in God is true joy." *Alfred A. Montapert*. Well,

you know how I love to sing and how I believe singing is a simple joy that gives happiness continually. The second part of this quote is the real deal, however. Being wrapped in the love of the Lord is a blanket of happiness that keeps me warm every day.

280. Happy people focus on the good things that have transpired in the past. When looking back on faded friendships or relationships, I always think about all of the good times that were experienced. Unhappy people, contrarily, focus on the bad. What good does that do? Nothing good is going to come out of that. Living for today, planning for tomorrow, and enjoying the pleasant memories of yesteryears, is how to live every day.

281. "The art of being happy lies in the power of extracting happiness from common things." *Henry Ward Beecher*. There is nothing more important than this, along with a positive mental attitude, toward living a rich and happy life. Not a single thing. Singing along when your favorite oldie comes on the radio, watching cartoons with the kids, feeding

the birds in the park, and a billion more, are "common things" that we can all delight in.

282. Brotherhood is not just a word out of the Lions Club or Theta Chi handbooks. Brotherhood and the belief, support, and love of our fellow man insures much happiness for all of us. Really think about that word today — Brotherhood. It is very powerful and hopefully, a word that you will seal in your heart.

283. We are all of one race, "The Human Race." I have said this hundreds of times in the "Mr. Happy" talks I've been fortunate to do. We have to get over the divisiveness that those with bitter hearts work to insure stays alive. I am going to vow to work every day with this thought in mind. Although we are all individuals, we are all one people, and one race.

284. "It isn't what you have or who you are, or where you are, or what you are doing that makes you happy or unhappy...it is what you think about." *Dale Carnegie.* Here again the master of happiness reinforces what is the real secret of happiness. I sometimes catch myself

being irritated, ticked-off at the guy who just cut me off on the highway, or the neighbor's dog "pooping on my grass." So what? That moment of irritation is taking away from the goodness I want to experience in life. It is not worth it, so for-get-about-it.

285. I learned that you can tell a lot about a man by the way he handles these three things: a rainy day, lost luggage, and tangled Christmas tree lights. We learn more about a person's true character when they are struggling with adversity than when they're on top of the world.

286. I have heard many people tell me I am the most blessed person they know because of my continual (well not continual; ask my assistant *Lynda* in the office, but "fairly" continual), state of happiness. The bottom line is I see all the good, deal with the bad, and go about living a rich life. If you know of a better way to live life, please let me know.

287. "You must try to generate happiness within yourself. If you aren't happy in one place, chances are you won't be happy anyplace."

Ernie "Let's play two" Banks. Mr. Chicago Cub himself. I am many times astounded when going out for an evening of fun with a group, when, as soon as we sit down, it happens. Someone belts out, "This place is boring, let's go someplace else." Don't fall for it. When I got in the car with my friends, I was already at "perfect speed" by being in their company. So like Mr. Cub said, tell 'em we are playing, we are having fun, and we might just "play two."

288. The following several "happyisms" that I want to share are about LOVE. These quotes are all from children; the oldest is 8. Love and happiness go hand in hand. If you really love yourself, not self-absorbed, but in a meaningful way, you will have the love of others first at hand. "Love is in the room with you at Christmas if you stop opening presents and listen." *Bobby-age 7.*

289. "When my grandma got arthritis, she couldn't bend over and paint her toenails anymore. So my grandpa does it for her now all the time,

even when his hands have arthritis, too. That's love." ***Rebecca-age 8.***

290. "If you want to learn to love better, start with a friend you hate." ***Nikka-age 6.*** That really is a lesson and there are not many other things in this book, or any book on happiness, that could say it better than Nikka has.

291. "Love is when Mommy sees Daddy smelly and sweaty and still says he is handsomer than Robert Redford." ***Chris-age 7.*** When people see us at our worst, not physically, but when we say and do things we regret and they still love us, "That's the good stuff."

292. "Love is when your puppy licks your face even after you left him alone all day." ***Mary Ann-age 4.*** A person that loves you even when you have beaten them with the golden rule as opposed to treating them with it as it applies, is a person with a golden heart. I want that person as my best friend.

293. "Love is when Mommy gives Daddy the best piece of chicken." ***Elaine-age 5.*** I always remember my Mama, when there were not

enough chicken legs to go around, always being the one who decided that she really wasn't that hungry after all. Is there any greater display of love than that? Thanks, Mama, and I love you.

294. Speaking of mamas, there is an old Jewish proverb that says "God could not be everywhere, that is why he created Mothers." Now that, my friends, is a happy thought for today and any day.

295. "It seemed like a good idea at the time." *Donald "Woody" Martin.* Another college buddy from Pittsburgh, now living in French Creek, W.Va. Woody is always sending me bits of wisdom from him and his Uncle Earl. There is a fine line between being spontaneous and happy about doing something, and doing something flat-out foolish. Go ahead; take a walk on the wild side, but keep your head on, for the love of Pete.

296. "A problem well stated is a problem half solved." *Henry Rischitelli.* Henry was a fraternity brother with me at WVWC and currently a successful businessman in

Atlanta. This nails it. If we would step back from our dilemma and clearly state what the problem is, we could always fix it in half the time and usually with a better end result.

297. "In negotiations you must be willing to lose in order to win." *Henry Rischitelli.* Another one from "Hammerin' Hank." Again, "Hank" nails this well-thought-out quote. If it is not a win-win situation then someone is getting taken advantage of. Happy people don't screw over others…period! Don't forget to ask me to tell you about the time he passed out on the table when the nurse pricked his finger to test his blood during a fraternity blood drive. I kid you not. He passed out from a finger prick. Oh, noooooooo…we didn't kid him about that, no way…yea, right!

298. "You have two ears and one mouth; use them proportionately." *Mark Biddle.* A fellow Theta Chi and here Mark gives a pearl of wisdom that we have all heard with different slants a million times. Why is it so many people don't get it? And…many times I am guilty of this

too. I am going to try even harder today to be a better listener. Thanks, Mark.

299. Don't wish away your life! We start when we are kids, wanting to sit at the grown-up table at Thanksgiving, then we want to be 13 so we can be teenagers, then 16 for our driver's license, then 18 so we can vote, then 21 so we can really be considered adult and then… the Lord only knows. That is all fine, as those are landmarks of growing up, but wishing away time for the sake of getting away from work or a spot we may not like the best is senseless. Life is way too short to wish it away. Let's wish that we make every minute good in some way, every day.

300. Be happy for others. It is sad to see someone who cannot find joy in the happiness of others. No need to elaborate, as we all know what I am talking about. A real pillar in the strength of a happy life is rejoicing in the good fortune of others, especially those we hold close. Be quick, in fact the first, to let them know how proud you are of their achievements. It will lift you as sky-high as the person who scored.

301. Just when you think it is over, the best is yet to come. My back hurts a lot more than it used to. I am starting to lose my hair. I have a much harder time exercising and I have to take cholesterol medication. Wa-Wa-Wa-Wa-WAAAAAAAAA. Give me a break. We have a big chunk of an exciting adventure that is just beginning. Life, as glorious as it has been, even with the toe stubs and heartbreaks, is just getting ready to break out. Saddle up and get ready to ride because you ain't seen nothin' yet.

302. Keeping your priorities in the proper order is one of the most important things you can ever do. Of course, sometimes you have to miss your kid's ball game because of another commitment, or you can't be home for the surprise party. On the other hand, there is no excuse for missing them all. My dad only saw me wrestle one time in 12 years. ONE time! A few years before he died, he apologized and said his "priorities were not where they should have been." We can't make up for missing yesterday but we

can darn well make sure we know where to focus our attention today.

303. "It's a small world, but I wouldn't want to paint it." *Greg "The Marauder" Mezzacapo, via Comedian Stephen Wright.* Most of us have heard of Steven Wright, the zany, dry, deadpan comedian with hair like Larry from the Three Stooges. Greg, on the other hand, was my roommate my senior year in college, along with a guy nicknamed "Beak," because…well you can take a guess. He would throw this line out with precise timing, and everyone would howl. Makes sense though, doesn't it? There is only so much work, play, volunteering, and all of the other stuff I can do each day. I'll paint what I can today and worry about tomorrow, tomorrow.

304. "You have to expect a few losses in a big operation." *Dan "Needle" Herod.* Dan's (another college chum; did I hang out with some insightful dudes or what?) Dad used to tell him this. Boy oh boy, is this ever true. Obviously in war, our soldiers pay the ultimate sacrifice for the good of the operation. We are all grateful, beyond words, for their

sacrifices. In a smaller context, we all struggle with day-to-day challenges. We can't expect to breeze right through them without taking some "losses." Those bruises, time delays, and inconveniences are all going to come. By expecting them we are ready for them and ultimately deal with them effectively.

305. "It is not enough to be good if you have the ability to be better, and it is not enough to be very good if you have the ability to be great." *J. B. Kennedy.* J.B is a hometown boy from Buckhannon, W.Va., and a college friend. His parents were always good to me when I lived in Buckhannon. He said an eighth grader wrote this. When we have given less than our best, regardless of the outcome of our efforts, the result is less than euphoric. When we give all that we can, even in defeat, we feel a sense of achievement.

306. "You can't make chicken salad out of chicken-doo." *Steve "Step and Fetch" Toth.* Yup, another WVWC boy. Yes, we have all heard this before, only with slightly different verbiage. It is so important that if we want a first-class job we have to have first-class ingredients,

whether it be building a company or building a house, building an organization or building a dinner menu. If we expect to end up with steak and lobster, we can't start with chipped beef on toast.

307. I have a friend of over 30 years that is more than special. He and I went to college together, fraternity brothers, were roommates off and on many times in our lives and he visits me for a week nearly every summer. His name is **Michael "Moon" Mullins.** He has given me so much wisdom over the years, and he contributed several great "Happy" sayings to this book. I want to share three: "It is better to light a candle than to curse the darkness"… "If things (or others) go wrong, don't go with them"… and "If you insist on killing time, try working it to death." Thanks, Moon, you really are the best. I am going to try harder on all three of these.

308. "Without vision, the people perish" **Proverbs 29:18.** I have said a million times that God never promised us tomorrow so it is so important to live for today. That does not mean

we don't look out on the horizon and plan for the sunrise and the joy another day will bring. Without a vision and hope for tomorrow, today will be an empty shell. Living for today, however, while planning for tomorrow, is the only way to be.

309. "Success is not forever and failure isn't fatal." ***Bill Struble.*** Bill is the head football coach and alumnus at our college, West Virginia Wesleyan, a fraternity brother, and still married to our fraternity sweetheart Jenny. He knows a great deal about both success and failure. He endured several losing seasons only to rebound and win the conference title three consecutive years. He also set the school record for the most wins ever by a football coach. Here's to you, Bill, and believing your quote. I am never going to forget either part.

310. "It is not enough to stare up the steps… we must step up the stairs." ***Bill Struble.*** Another pearl of wisdom from West Virginia Wesleyan's college football coach. This is as simple as it gets. All of the preparation in the world won't get the job done. We have

to jump in with both feet, get a little dirt on our hands and get to it. It takes another job off of the table and makes us feel good about gettin' it done.

311. "Decide on what you think is right, and stick to it." *George Eliot.* I love people that stand by their convictions, even when I may not agree with them. There are way too many people who flow with what the in-crowd is feeling. Stand up for what you believe. You can still listen to opposing views, but, unless you are wrong, trust your heart and stand firm. People will come around and respect you for it.

312. **"What can be added to the happiness of a man who is in health, out of debt and has a clear conscience?"** *Adam Smith.*

313. Make sure you have a good relationship with a banker, a lawyer, an accountant, a financial advisor, a dentist, a doctor, a mechanic, an electrician and a plumber. You should use and have a sense of trust with each of these individuals. Every one of these people will make you very sad, or very angry at one part of your life. If you do not trust them, strongly,

then find another one. Side note: Please do not wait until you need one, when the pipes have broken and your house is flooding, to find one.

314. Giving an allowance as opposed to having children "earn" it is a recipe for disaster. I received my first allowance when I was in sixth grade. I was required to make my bed, clean my room and cut the grass. It was 1969 and it was 50 cents a week. It taught me two things — nothing is free and it feels good to carry a share of the weight in the family. Children will not understand either of those feelings with a handout. Nor will they ever learn to do their own laundry. Think about that for a minute.

315. Learn how to appreciate a compliment. When someone says "good job," "your hair looks great" or "Wow, this is the best chicken casserole I have ever stuck my fork in," say "Thank you." Nothing else really needs to be said.

316. "After last night's slaughter in Pittsburgh, look at today's disappointment like it is

tomorrow's opportunity." ***Bill "Wilber" McMinn.*** Dateline Monday, January 24, 2005. Blue skies in Virginia Beach while a thunderstorm of despair lay heavy throughout western Pennsylvania. Bill, a true best friend, was kind enough to share this cheerful thought (a touch of sarcasm here) after his beloved Pittsburgh Steelers were beaten by the New England Patriots, like a red-headed rug-rat, to earn a seat in "Loserville," population, them. Sorry, Steeler fans. Seriously, what a great way to look at things. We can whine about a loss or pick ourselves up and get ready to play again tomorrow. I love that. Thanks Bill, maybe next year.

317. As important as first impressions are, they can trick you. I am very trusting and believe that most people should be. That is not to say I am foolish. I give people the benefit of the doubt. If you don't, you end up being so cautious that you lose the beauty of people. Be attentive to the second and third times you see folk, so that the first impression was the real McCoy.

318. I do not believe in tipping 20% or even 15% for inattentive or, God forbid, rude service. On the other hand, I do not blame the server for bad food. It is not their fault so don't take it out on them. I don't make a scene, but I will bring it to the manager's attention. This goes back to rewarding bad behavior. On the flip side, I will give a large tip when someone does something so above and beyond that they deserve it. It's as simple as that.

319. Screaming never solves anything. An exception to this is in letting the players know how proud you are of them for winning the big game. Screaming all too often gets ugly. Someone is trying to shout over the other and many times an argument ensues. Arguments lead to name calling, profanities, and fights. I do not want any part of any of this. Let the other person yell, or simply walk away. A screamer can't scream for long…screaming at themselves.

320. "Perseverance is a great element of success. If you only knock long enough at the gate, you are sure to wake up somebody." *Longfellow.* I love this, from one of the greats. I remember

playing the children's card game "Authors," as a child and he was one of the big guys. It is rare that a continued knock will go unanswered. That is not to say with an answer that we wish for, but an answer nonetheless. Keep knockin'!

321. "A person who says it cannot be done should not interrupt the person doing it." *Chinese Proverb*. Be the encourager, or better yet, the one who jumps in to help. Regardless of the outcome, you will have made two people happy that day.

322. "Man has never made any material as resilient as the human spirit." *Bernard Williams*. The ability of man to snap back from the most devastating of circumstances is mind-numbing to me. I like to think I keep on a keepin' on, but I cannot wipe the shoes of the likes of *Helen Keller*, *Nelson Mandela*, or *Senator John McCain*. Their stories and their spirits are what inspire me and encourage me to be a better person every day.

323. "There are many ways to measure success, not the least of which is the way your child

describes you in talking to a friend." I have no idea who said this, but I would imagine there are few rays of sunshine brighter than to hear your son or daughter telling a playmate what a king or queen you are. They see everything you do, except for your mistakes.

324. "I think the purpose of life is to be useful, to be responsible, to be honorable, to be compassionate. It is, after all, to matter, to count, to stand for something, to have made some difference that you have lived at all." **Leo C. Rosten.** I have spun this theme several times in this book, my favorite said previously by **William James**. I believe with all of my soul that life is to be spent on something that outlasts it. How about you?

325. "There are no shortcuts to anyplace worth going." **Beverly Sills.** Isn't this the truth? Half-steppin' or cutting the job short only leaves you with the short end of the stick. Worse yet, the end result is you feel like you've been beaten with that stick. Don't cut it short. If you don't have time, stop the job and pick it up again another day.

326. "Most of us miss out on life's big prizes. The Nobel. The Pulitzer. The Oscars. The Tonys. The Emmys. But we are all eligible for life's small pleasures. A pat on the back. A kiss behind the ear. A four-pound bass. A full moon. An empty parking space. A cracklin' fire. A great meal. A glorious sunset. Hot soup. Cold beer." *Anonymous.*

327. "Life should not be a journey to the grave with the intention of arriving safely in a well-preserved body, but rather to skid in sideways, body thoroughly used up, worn out and screaming "YOO-HOO What a ride!" My good buddy Chad is one of the hardest working people I know. He and his wife, Sheila, built a business from the ground up and today it is a multi-million dollar corporation. They gave me this quote and it makes me laugh out loud everytime I read it. Life is meant to be lived. Don't take this wrong. Life is not to be abused, but respected, lived, and loved. Thanks for the ride, Chad and Sheila.

328. **"The fog leaves when the son/sun shines in."**

329. Here's a two-for-one from two legends. "There are two ways of exerting one's strength: one is pushing down, the other is pulling up." Booker T. Washington. "A champion is someone who gets up when he can't." Jack Dempsey.

330. Think about this as you drive to work this morning. The length of your life has little to do with the quality of your life. LIVING and GIVING are two of the biggest keys to a happy life.

331. A broken heart is worth the price of admission. As painful as a heart that has been torn in two is for all of us, and believe me, I have had my share, it has always been worth the ride that preceded it. Don't ever be afraid to have your heart broken.

332. Sit up straight. Walk upright and at a brisk pace. You could write a book about someone by how they carry themselves. What does a slouch tell you? How about a lazy, haphazard walk? An alert posture and quick step gives

the feeling and appearance of confidence, and a person who is to be respected.

333. We have talked and will continue to talk a great deal about children. Children just lend themselves to happiness. They are vessels waiting to be filled. I believe if they are filled with love from the heart, respect from the soul, and loyalty to the core, the values you have instilled in them will last forever. If you don't have any kids, go play with the neighbors.

334. Get a good dictionary and keep it in arms' reach. I just bought a nice one. I got tired of the paperback knobby-eared one that I had. My buddy Shep Davis has a huge one on his coffee table in his living room. It is inspirational. We play word games, and the "Mac-Daddy" dictionary always has the final say. Plus, it is just nice to browse through over coffee.

335. "Class is the aura of confidence that is being sure without being cocky. Class has nothing to do with money. Class never runs scared. It is self-discipline and self-knowledge. It is the sure-footedness that comes with having proved that you can meet life." *Ann Landers.*

We all know the sisters Ann and Abby have solved more of America's dilemmas than all of the politicians combined. This is one of my favorites of their thousands. You can't hide class or fake it, so don't.

336. "Failure is the opportunity to begin again, more intelligently." *Henry Ford.* Here is another spin on an old favorite. Maybe this will be the one that reinforces to you the inevitability of mistakes, and the opportunity successful people grasp from them. On another note, wouldn't you like to have one of Henry's old Fords just to tool around town in?

337. "Do an Affirmation." *Ray "never a hair out of place" Mesing.* A friend of over 30 years from Pittsburgh. Good dude! He drops a note, out of the clear blue, to someone he cares about. He lets them know two or three things that he values in their friendship. It reinforces their relationship and maybe caught the other person at just the time when they needed a boost. This is a good one. Thanks Ray.

338. Live a good, honorable life. Then when you get older and think back, you will be able to enjoy it a second time.

339. Always leave a light on. How warm is it to come home to a light inviting you in? "Hi, welcome home, you have been missed." It is a very simple pleasure of life. Always leave the porch light on for your kids or guests. It makes them feel welcome and safe.

340. Today is THE day! Everything that we have talked about throughout this book, everything that you know in your heart to be true and right, everything that all of us know will make us better and happier people. We need to begin. Don't try to try to eat the whole pie at once; just start with a slice. Cut back or better yet, QUIT smoking, walk around the block, go to church, fix coffee for your assistant, attend the civic league meeting — all of these things, one at a time. Life is good and will be better.

341. Go walking in the rain…with the one you love or all by yourself. It really is a good feeling catching a warm summer shower. I get caught in the rain on my pontoon boat a couple of

times a year. As long as there is no lightning, it is a wonderful experience. Don't forget to jump in the puddles. Come on, you're still a kid at heart.

342. "It's nice to be important, but it's important to be nice." ***Bryan "Sir Nose" Armstrong.*** One of the nicest people I have ever met in my life. Bryan and I lived together in college and at our first jobs in Myrtle Beach, S.C. He would send my Mom a Mother's Day card when I would forget. Just disgustingly nice. This quote is so simple, it is silly. I love it and wish we could all practice this daily. "Beak," you are the man.

343. There are very few successful people in the world that are not enthusiastic. Not just about their jobs, but about life. They get excited about everything — the kids' game, extra cheese on the pizza, grilling on the back deck, the first snowfall, the ice cream truck, and heading to the office in the morning. Success seems to breed confidence, good manners, a smile, and respect. Success starts with enthusiasm.

344. We all have heard the saying "God helps those who help themselves." There are two Bible verses that are a couple of my favorites that I believe parallel this thought. Hopefully they will be meaningful to you as well. "With God, all things are possible." *Matthew 19:26.* "I can do all things through Christ who strengthens me." *Philippians 4:13.*

345. "Love Helps Those, Who Cannot Help Themselves." *Paul Overstreet.* Here again is a great saying by my favorite country singer and songwriter. As I stated before, this guy, I guarantee, will make you happy. This is off his first album, "Sowin' Love," released in 1989. Go grab a copy today, plug it in to the car stereo and let me know what you think. No kidding, it is moving stuff.

346. One of the single most influential things you can do to make yourself feel great is to help someone that needs it, *before* they have to ask. From helping an elderly lady put the groceries in her car, to finding a lost mitten of a child at the bus stop, there are few things

I can think of that makes life better than a simple act of kindness.

347. "You were born an original; don't die a copy." I have no idea who said this, but it is very good. They say imitation is the greatest form of flattery and I believe that. If you see something that is working for someone else then by all means copy it. It is very important, however, to develop your own style and uniqueness.

348. Commitment is everything. If there are only a couple of ideas in this book that move you, and you commit to making them a part of your life, your life will be better, starting today. Just pick a single thing, and commit to it.

349. Speaking of commitment, pick three or four things that you resolve to begin. Write them down on a small index card and tape it to the inside of your medicine cabinet. Read them the first thing every morning and you will be much more inclined to stay committed to them. This is an easy one you can start right now.

350. This is more of a practical "Happyism," but it will mean a great deal to your family. Write a will and plan your funeral. I have been involved many times when no will and no plans were made. It is a mess, and a terrible strain on the family, as somebody will have to make these heart-wrenching decisions. It is best to call an attorney, but you can do a will yourself on a piece of paper, have it witnessed and notarized, and you are good to go (no pun intended). Doing this will take a weight off of your shoulders.

351. Things always take longer than we expect them to. Trips, jobs, meeting, well… anything. Anticipate this and you will avoid a big chunk of disappointment. Fixing the kitchen sink takes me roughly as long as it took to build the Panama Canal, but I already know that, so I just plan on having my shaving kit with me.

352. There is a book called "The Complete Life's Little Instruction Book." It is written by *H. Jackson Brown Jr.* and published by Rutledge Hill Press. It is fantastic. I would like to meet Mr. Brown and thank him for such a wonderful compilation of wit and wisdom

on the majority of life's questions. I keep a copy in my nightstand drawer. Go get one and you will too.

353. #1473 from "The Complete Life's Little Instruction Book" is this: "Ask yourself if what you're doing today is getting you closer to where you want to be tomorrow." That just kind of says it all.

354. Learn a simple blessing that you can say over a meal. It is a great joy to me to say grace for all of the blessings that God has bestowed upon my family and friends. What a simple way to express a sense of gratitude. No speeches are necessary. This is not about you. It is about being grateful.

355. "Try not to become a success, but rather try to become a man of value." *Albert Einstein.* A familiar theme and a statement that makes me feel good. All the success in the world will escape our grasp if we do not know what our values are and then live them.

356. "Lord, grant that I may always desire more than I can accomplish." *Michelangelo.* I want

to leave this earth with a plate of chores, and a hundred items on my wish list that still need attending to. Every time we take care of something, why don't we add another item to the bottom of the list?

357. Rejoice in birth. Maybe they are in your family, maybe in the office, or maybe just a beautiful child born to a stranger. A miracle has just arrived. Take a moment and appreciate the splendor. If you can, drop a note, or if they are close friends, buy the child a share of Disney stock in his or her name and send them the certificate. Or...as I mentioned before, plant a tree in the parent's yard.

358. If you can't be kind, at least have the decency to be vague. However, being genuine is always the best course.

359. "Women and music should never be dated." **Goldsmith**. Ah! This is beyond simply profound. The good ones just get better with age.

360. "It's Impossible." Besides being a great song by **Perry Como** (who incidentally, had the best

male voice to ever set foot on this planet), it is a statement of sheer folly. Nothing is impossible. All of the great achievements of society were, at one time, considered impossible. Don't ever get caught up in believing "It's Impossible."

361. Now, if we have to talk about burdens, and I guess we should… "If I hold it for a minute, that's not a problem. If I hold it for an hour, I'll have an ache in my right arm. If I hold it for a day, you'll have to call an ambulance. In each case, it's the same weight, but the longer I hold it, the heavier it becomes." Set your burden down and look at it tomorrow in the light of a new day.

362. Watch the stars. Get a telescope and a star map to go with it. You can always find one at a yard sale. Go out on your deck, patio, or park and try to find the "Big Dipper." Better still, when there is a report of a rare astrological occurrence, even if it is in the middle of the night, set your alarm and get up to see it. It may not happen again, as they always say, for another 10,000 years.

363. I believe more than ever we reap what we sow, good things happen to good people and we sleep in the bed that we make. The "good life" that we all strive for will be more easily attained if we start each day with the basic premise that we will be good to our fellow man and ourselves.

364. Well, this book is nearly complete and I thought this would be a good place to add this. I heard someone once say that the key to successful living is to practice that success every day. Now, that makes solid sense to me. All of the happy thoughts that I have shared with you in this book will not make a dent in your life if you do not practice them each and every day.

365. Never underestimate the power of prayer. I try to start each day thanking the Lord for another chance to be a good person this day. I also stop and ask for guidance when I am struggling for an answer or am just plain scared. Lastly, when a tragedy is upon anyone, a moment of prayer to ask God to intervene is a powerful tool.

366. Well, this is it. I hope you enjoyed the ride. This is the "leap year" day. I said I was going to list a few of my favorite songs and maybe some of you may want to grab a copy of them. In no particular order, they are: 1)"Autumn Leaves" and "'Til Then" by the Mills Brothers, 2) "Fly Me to the Moon" and "Just the Way You Look Tonight" by Frank Sinatra, 3) "Seein' my Father in Me" and "The Richest Man on Earth" by Paul Overstreet, 4) "The Boys are Back in Town" by Thin Lizzy, 5) "Ain't that a Kick in the Head" and "Everybody Loves Somebody, Sometime" by Dean Martin. This is the first song I learned when I started piano lessons. 6) "It's Impossible" and "And I Love You So" by Perry Como 7) "American Pie" and "Castles in the Air" by Don McClean, 8) "Cowboy Christmas" and "Cowboy Logic" by Michael Martin Murphy 9) "Forever and Ever Amen" and "There Always be a Honky-Tonk Somewhere" by Randy Travis, 10) "He Stopped Loving Her Today" by George Jones, 11) "Hold Me, Thrill Me, Kiss Me" by Mel Carter, 12) "Set 'em Up Joe" and "Is it Raining at Your House" by Vern "The Voice" Gosdin, 13) "I Wish a Buck was Still Silver" by Merle

Haggard, 14) "This Could be the Start of Something Big" by Steve Lawrence and Eydie Gorme, 15) "The Wonder of You" by Elvis, 16) "America the Beautiful" by anybody, 17) "P-Funk and Flashlight" by "Parliament," 18) "The Ride" by David Allen Coe, 19) "Amarillo by Morning" and "I Can Still Make Cheyenne" by George Strait, 20) "The Bear Necessities" by Baloo the Bear from the movie, "The Jungle Book." Ya' just don't get acting like Baloo these days.

J. P. "GUS" GODSEY
Named the "Happiest Man in America"
by USA Weekend magazine

USA Weekend magazine named J.P. "Gus" Godsey the "happiest man in America" on March 7, 2003. Martin E.P. Seligman, Ph.D., author of "Authentic Happiness: Using the New Positive Psychology to Realize Your Potential for Lasting Fulfillment" and nationally recognized happiness expert, worked with USA Weekend to identify J.P. as the happiest person. J.P. underwent a number of tests that measured his current level of happiness, satisfaction with his family life, work life, level of optimism and a host of other characteristics that reveal happiness. J.P. scored in the top percentile of 70,000 Americans who have taken this series of tests.

J. P. Godsey is currently a vice president of investments with Ferris, Baker Watts, Inc. His client focus is helping retirees (and those within 10 years of retiring) in making appropriate financial plans to insure their "Golden Years" are golden. J. P. graduated with a bachelor of science degree in business management and economics from West

Virginia Wesleyan College. He is a certified senior advisor in investments, and is a graduate assistant in Dale Carnegie training. He has been a licensed securities broker and financial advisor for over 20 years. He also serves on his college alumni board, West Virginia Wesleyan College, and on his international fraternity board, Theta Chi. He serves as the president of Earning by Learning, is a founding member of the Richard Hassell Foundation, is a member of the Juvenile Diabetes Research Foundation, and is a Human Rights Commissioner for the City of Virginia Beach.

J.P. is involved in many community organizations including the Thanksgiving and holiday food and toy drives he started 20 years ago. He received the 2000 Human Rights Award from the City of Virginia Beach, and is the past chairman of the Republican Party of Virginia Beach. J. P. serves on the Beach Events Steering Committee and is an active member of the Wolfsnare Civic League. He is also a director of the Mills Brothers International Society and coordinates the annual Mills Brothers benefit concerts benefitting various foundations in Virginia Beach. J.P. is a director of the Irving "Blueprint" Parker Leadership Foundation, and raises money for various political candidates and for the Joy Fund Thanksgiving Football Bowl that provides funds for underprivileged children in the Hampton Roads area. J. P. was also chosen as one of America's Outstanding Young Men for several consecutive years in the 1980s.

J.P.'s first book "How To Be Happy Every Day" was released April 1, 2005. This insightful and humorous book offers ways to find more happiness in life on a daily basis. It is available at fine bookstores, on the Internet, and at J.P.'s Web site www.MrHappy USA.com.

Most recently and with the encouragement of friends, J.P. started **"The MrHappyUSA Foundation."** : This exciting project's focus will be on "Elder Abuse" that has been called the "Silent Terror" among our senior citizens. Please go to the www.MrHappyUSA.com Web site to see how you can be involved.

CONTACT INFORMATION

J.P. has given over 100 presentations over the last 4 years can't wait to speak to you. He would like to join you at your next event to speak with your corporate group, association or to help promote your event or product. His talks are always "tailor made" to the group he is addressing. "Gus" obviously knows a great deal about happiness, but he also helps a group focus on getting more out of themselves, life and their relationships. You can count on a high energy, humorous talk that brings specific points to the group that they can use TODAY. Your group will leave the meeting on a higher plane of success then when they came in. Contact "Gus" today at www.MrHappyUSA.com or through his publicist Rick Frishman, the President of "Planned TV Arts," at www.RickFrishman.com or call Rick at 212/593-5845.

~ THE J.P. GODSEY SHOW ~

Every Wednesday afternoon from 4-5 PM, "The J. P. Godsey Show" is heard throughout Greater Hampton Roads on the 20,000 watt "blowtorch," 670 AM WPMH. Drive home with J. P. as he interviews cutting edge guests that are today's hottest newsmakers.

This upbeat, informative and off the wall show covers it all. From current political crises, to the latest sports star, to the celebrity du'jour, "The J.P. Godsey Show" will keep you glued to the dial. Each week, join "Gus" for fascinating conversations. In fact, join in by calling 757-465-6700. If he isn't asking the questions that you want, you can ask them yourself. Or… e-mail your questions to <u>talktogus@ MrHappyUSA.com</u>.

From Washington to Hollywood, from Mo-Town to downtown, don't miss "The J.P. Godsey Show" each Wednesday from 4-5 PM on 670 AM WPMH. The show that makes everybody HAPPY!

THE MrHappyUSA FOUNDATION

Gus, along with several of his friends, has recently founded **"The MrHappyUSA Foundation."** The Foundation will focus on the needs of seniors particularly "Elder Abuse," which has been called "The Silent Terror." The foundation's aim will be to combat abuse at all levels.

This is an exciting and unique opportunity to help those that are battling terrible environments.

Please go to the www.MrHappyUSA.com Web site for additional information. Tax deductible contributions can be made directly to the foundation to:

The MrHappyUSA FOUNDATION
c/o The Virginia Beach Foundation
P.O. Box 4629
Virginia Beach, VA 23454

A portion of the proceeds from the sale of this book will go to support **"The MrHappyUSA Foundation."**

Please join us and thank you for your support.

"Giving back always means getting back...many times over."

Come on, get on with it, I got me some cake to eat.

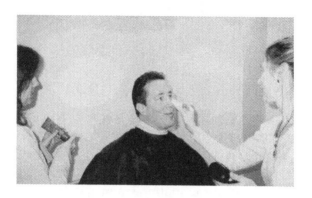

This is me getting pancake batter on my face before "Good Morning America" or "Tonight with Connie Chung." Man, I am glad I don't have to do this every day.

Here I am sharing a laugh with Dr. Martin Seligman. He is the guy who gave me all of the happy tests and when I scored at the top of the list, he said, "You really are a happy freak." Dr. Marty is a real nice man.

*Dancing with a balloon on the boardwalk during
the USA Weekend Magazine photo shoot.
How pathetic am I!*

*My sister Sue, my brother P. J. and me. I'm
the little one with a diaper on, the size of a
hubcap. My grandmother "Mo-Mo," (Swedish
for Mother's-Mother) is seated in the rear. She
had 14 children and was in her 80s when this
picture was taken, I guess around 1959.*

*This is your old-fashioned, standard,
run-of-the-mill, press release photo. I
cannot look any cheesier if I tried.*

*The boys at Zoufaly beach in Connecticut, from the
left, Dennis, Greg, Bryan, Gus, and Steve.*

*The night before I was on "Good Morning America"
a bunch of the boys from college met me in the city for
dinner. There was more love at that table for three hours
than many people experience in a lifetime. I am a lucky
man. Clockwise from the magazine, Joe Z., Susan, Lisa,
Dicky, Dennis, Robin, Greg, Klebs, and Gus.*

*I was honored to speak at the Mt. Zion African Methodist
Episcopal Church here in Virginia Beach on Easter Sunday
2004, by the Pastor and great friend, the Rev. Bill Dyson.*

*Gus with Rulon Gardner, US Olympic Heavyweight
Gold and Bronze Medlist in Greco-Roman Wrestling.
Rulon is holding up a copy of Gus's book and is
actually quoted on page v.*

*The "Okie from Muskogee" himself, Merle Haggard. I
had a chance to meet him before a show at the Little Creek
Amphibious Naval Base. Nice man, extremely patriotic
and a country music legend.*

*Here with basketball coaching legend, Charles "Lefty" Driesell
having lunch at Fredrico's in Virginia Beach. Wow, what a
great place to eat. "Lefty" is in the basketball hall of fame and
the fourth winningest coach in college history.*

*This was a welcome home party the City of Virginia Beach
threw for me when I got back from doing all the TV shows in
New York. It was humbling. All my friends were there. My
sister and brother even flew in from Indy. From left, my sister
Sue, Gil Davis, and me. Gil Davis is a very good friend and
the smartest guy I have ever met. He was the attorney who
represented Paula Jones against President Bill Clinton.*

My best buddy from college, Bryan "Beak" Armstrong, and me in 1981. He and I ran the "2001 VIP Club" together in Myrtle Beach, S.C., and had more fun than a little bit. We played football at the beach all day and worked until 3 or 4 a.m. every night. I get tired even thinking about that now.

Here he is, the man himself, Mr. Paul Overstreet. One of the greatest songwriters of all time. I got this pic with him back in '91 or '92 after he appeared at Regent University here at the Beach. Is that the biggest cheese eatin' smile you've ever seen? I was happy!

162

Garth Brooks was at the top of every chart in the world when I met him backstage in Richmond, Va., in '94. GREAT guy. The nicest entertainer I have ever met. We took this shot and immediately went to our seats. He had already changed clothes and was walking out on stage before we had sat down. He is wearing the Suffolk, VA sweatshirt and yes... that is MY hat I am wearing.

Everybody looks at this shot, and just smiles. All of my best buddies from college at a summer cookout in Connecticut in '86 or '87. Clockwise from Uncle Buck (he is the guy with sunglasses-front left), Carmine, Dicky (with his mouth open in the back), Batman, Mezz (biting someone's hand), Dennis (I think that is his hand), Steve, Gus and Roy.

This is the only family picture we have. It was the last one taken, Thanksgiving 1999, before Mama died. This was the last time I was with her. Clockwise from Mama, Joel (P.J.'s youngest), Judi, Gus, Sue, Nathan (P.J.'s second), Doreen (P.J.'s wife), P.J., and Harmony (P.J's oldest).

The Mills Brothers. The greatest vocal group in the history of music. Look closely and you can see this is autographed to Gus. It was taken, probably in the 1940s, and autographed to some guy named Gus. My sister got it for me on eBay. Pretty cool, huh?

164

*This is a high school basketball team my Dad coached.
He is in the front middle. I have no idea who they are or
when it was taken. If anybody knows, please call me.*

*1982, Myrtle Beach, running the 2001/VIP Club, and
hanging out with Roger Maris and Mickey Mantle.
Honestly, does it get much better than that? Like anybody
else my age, they were both childhood idols. We brought
them both to town for a charity golf tournament. They
were gentlemen and nice as could be. With us was my
girlfriend, Zade Turner. A nice lady too.*

This was my senior year, Theta Chi, West Virginia Wesleyan, and these are the guys that are still my best buddies today, nearly 30 years later. Check out the names, as you will hear from many of these guys throughout this book. Is it just me or do we look a little different now?

"Princess Di." You talk about royalty. This lady has interviewed six U.S. Presidents. She and Robin Roberts could not have been more gracious on the first big TV show I was on. It was real cool.

The sweetest lady I met in New York! Mrs. Chung was the one that held up on the air a jar of my homemade pasta sauce that I had given her prior to the show. That is how I ended up in the pasta sauce business. Thanks, Connie!

MY FIGHT WITH CANCER
(There ain't an easy street in sight)

I don't even remember the day, but it was around 9:00 in the morning. I was running late getting to the office. The phone rang as I was two steps away from the front door. It was the nurse who told me I had cancer. What???? I sat down.

My annual physical (see Happyism #68) showed something strange in my blood. My doctor referred me to an urologist a block down the street. That doctor told me it was all but guaranteed to be an infection. "Take these pills and come back in a month and we'll test you again. Everything will be jake."

A month later my blood was still bad. I had a biopsy. Trust me, that's no picnic in and of itself.

Three weeks after that is when I got that phone call; "You have prostate cancer. It is only in one spot and it is in a very early stage. We should be able to treat it." I went to four doctors and got four different opinions on what to do. Ironically, there are only four ways to treat prostate cancer, which goes to show you, nobody really knows what the heck they are talking about when it comes to cancer. It is just an educated guessing game.

Well, anyway, I had cryo surgery. This is where they freeze the cancer as opposed to cutting the whole prostate out. Six weeks later I went back, had another blood test and everything was supposed to be cool. NOT... last Monday my doctor called and said my PSA (that is the guide they use to check the level of your cancer with 1 being good and 10 being bad) was 9.6. Before I had the surgery my PSA was only 2.5. Now, since the surgery, it had almost quadrupled.

The doc said this sometimes happens; it 'in all probability' was just an infection due to the surgery. Take these antibiotics and come back in a month and we'll test your blood again. It will probably be back to normal."

I was stunned as I have heard this "in all probability" song before. So, when I say ya' gotta' control the controllables (check Happyism #168) I mean it. Stay tuned. Keep me in your prayers and I'll keep you posted.

Note: since this book was completed I had a follow up exam and my PSA is back down to 1.6. I am grateful but still watchful!